SIT STILL AND PROSPER

STEPHANIE GRIFFITHS, CFA

sit still and prosper

How a Former Money Manager Discovered the Path to Investing with Greater Clarity, Calmness, and Confidence

A BIRD IN
THE SKY

ISBN 978-1-99949-110-9 (paperback)
ISBN 978-1-99949-111-6 (ebook)

Produced by Page Two
www.pagetwostrategies.com
Cover and interior design by Taysia Louie
Editing by Paul Taunton
Proofreading by Alison Strobel

18 19 20 21 5 4 3 2 1

www.stephaniegriffiths.ca

To my teachers

Contents

Disclaimer

NOTHING IN THIS book is intended as investment advice, or advice of any kind. Please do your own research before making any financial decision. If you're uncertain about the best solution for you, consider investing in independent professional financial advice.

Additionally, please note that this book reflects the author's opinions about investing, meditation, and life at the time it was written. The information is believed to be correct and current at the time of writing, and best efforts have been made to check the facts. But errors and personal biases may remain: proceed with caution.

Finally, never forget the ten most-ignored words in the investment industry, brought to you by the US Securities and Exchange Commission: "Past performance is not a reliable indicator of future performance."

Introduction

A FEW YEARS AGO, a screenwriter friend emailed me asking for investment advice. Like many people, he has little interest in investing, but worries about his long-term financial security. The three hours I spent drafting a detailed reply were humbling. I was an expert, a former mutual fund manager with almost two decades of experience. But I'd never looked at my own industry through the eyes of a consumer. Every piece of advice I offered came with a caveat or exception that made my response read like a long-winded mash-up of "be careful" and "it depends." For all my supposed expertise, I was unable to carve out concise directions to help my friend safely navigate potentially shark-infested waters.

Four years later, I've written this book, which I believe to be the first investment guide by an author claiming no expertise, offering no advice. Here you'll find clear signposts steering you away from dangerous pitfalls, as well as plenty of practical information and encouragement. But no prescriptive, step-by-step recipe for success. That was the path I thought I was on when I began, as an expert with an encyclopedic list of rigid opinions. But as Zen master Shunryu Suzuki wrote, "In the beginner's mind there are many possibilities, while in the expert's there are few." Writing this book, I've learned a lot about behavioral biases, especially my own. I've also learned that no single solution is right for everyone. Today I believe that the best strategy is to open our minds to the full range of possibilities, check their references, then listen to our hearts. Not just in investing, but also in life.

This book aspires to introduce you to the latest generation of financial innovations, including robo-advisors, exchange-traded funds (ETFs), and fee-based fiduciary advice, while at the same time making a case for mindfulness as an investment strategy. Ultimately, though, it's up to you to decide what helps you sleep at night.

When I joined the investment industry in the mid-1990s, mutual funds were almost the only game in town, offering affordable professional money management to mainstream consumers. At the time, I had a journalism degree, a toddler, and a day-care bill as high as my rent. I studied for my Chartered Financial Analyst (CFA) exams nights and weekends, often wondering if I would pass all three before I passed out from exhaustion.

By 2013, the CFA exams were a distant memory. For more than fifteen years, I'd worked for the same firm, first as the assistant to a mutual fund manager, later as manager of a fund myself. My toddler had grown up, graduated high school, and dropped out of a prestigious US college. My second child was in private school. A workaholic, I wasn't complete without a briefcase full of paper, a Starbucks cup in one hand, and a BlackBerry in the other. Toward the end, I learned to meditate, jumping on the latest self-help bandwagon as a potential productivity tool. I had no interest in Buddhism, spirituality, or religion of any kind, unless you consider investing a religion. That was pretty much how I practiced it, and I was a hardcore fundamentalist. My way was the right way; everyone else was delusional.

Then, one damp day in April, my employer consolidated its product offerings. The fund I'd obsessed over for more than a decade got a new name and two new managers. Yet when I handed over my BlackBerry and headed for home, I felt strangely liberated. I figured I'd spend a few months enjoying my first real summer vacation in years, then look for a new fund to run when the weather turned.

For most of my career, I'd focused entirely on smaller North American stocks, a category that had become too expensive for my bargain-hunter taste. When I started looking outside my comfort zone, my mind was boggled by the multitude of options. In addition to thousands of traditional mutual funds, disruptive newcomers with catchy names and friendly personalities were popping up everywhere, promising to make investing simple, scientific, and perhaps even fun.

As I contemplated my own investment options with the luxury of free time, I dug deep into academic research I'd only skimmed in the past, topics including luck versus skill, human behavioral biases, and the impressive long-term track record of the humble index fund. I discovered that certain "facts" I'd taken as articles of faith were actually controversial, with solid academic research on both sides. Gradually, my fundamentalism melted away.

When fall came, I didn't return to the industry after all. Instead, for the next two years I travelled across North America exploring the frontiers of finance, meeting pioneers of innovative commonsense investment solutions. This book tells their stories as well as my own.

I hope you find them as inspiring as I do.

1

How the Dutch Conquered North America

HEAVY SHEETS OF ice-cold rain are falling on my head. It's late July, but feels more like January. I'm sitting on a horse in the middle of the warm-up ring at the Caledon Equestrian Festival. A groom runs to the tack shop to buy a raincoat. Not for me—I'm already soaked to the skin—but for Riley, the horse.

Named for the expression "living the life of Riley" (a carefree life of comfort at someone else's expense), Riley lived large for livestock. He had regular visits from a chiropractor, consumed quantities of expensive nutritional supplements, and due to his sensitive skin, wore calfskin jumping boots. An equine with a canine personality, his whole body lit up at the sight of a Starbucks cup or paper bag from McDonald's. He wasn't merely a pampered pet, however, but rather a talented athlete, the overpriced sports car of my middle age. He could gallop and leap around a course of jumps with amazing agility for a thousand-pound-plus junk-food addict. As a teenager, I'd dreamed of riding a horse like Riley, and now, after twenty years of office captivity, I was living the dream. For the summer, anyway.

Back when I was a money manager seeking to reduce the stress in my life, I had signed up for lessons in meditation, which were free, and horseback riding, which turned out to be hazardous to my wealth as well as my health. Cantering around a corner one night, Daisy, my riding-school rental, tripped on her own feet and fell, taking both of us down. I was lucky to limp away with mild whiplash. Clearly it was time to invest in a horse of my own—one with lower mileage and better safety features.

Riley was listed for sale on the website of a top show jumping stable. I suspected he was beyond my budget but sent a hopeful email. They offered me a test-drive and I fell in love. But his price was half-again more than my budget. His owner agreed to a lease-to-own deal, giving us a year to get to know each other.

My summer in the sun began that May with a freak blizzard at the first horse show of the season. The coach shouted into the bitter wind while I struggled to slow down. Riley, spooked by the pelting precipitation, galloped wildly around the jumps. Competitors with more sense stayed home, but this was my version of fantasy baseball camp, and I wasn't going to miss a minute of it. Even if I froze to death.

We were a great team—a recovering workaholic and a has-been child prodigy. Riley had an impressive pedigree, sharing a great-great-grandfather with 2008 Olympic gold medal winner Hickstead. Born in Amsterdam, Riley had arrived in Canada as a youngster, full of promise and potential. When I met him, he'd been benched for a season, recovering from a serious injury. Babysitting me for the summer was a perfect pit stop on his way back to the big leagues.

Today, the Netherlands is known for producing some of world's finest show jumpers, but back in the eighteenth century, Amsterdam was a global leader in financial innovation, the Wall Street of the world. As early as 1639, at least 360 different commodities were traded on the Amsterdam bourse.[1] (*Bourse* is a European term for stock exchange.) By the late 1700s, the Dutch were the kings of finance. They traded currencies, government bonds, futures, and options, as well as more exotic products such as securities backed by Washington, DC, real estate and annuities betting on the long lives of schoolgirls who had survived smallpox.[2]

With no SUVs, cruise vacations, or high-maintenance hobby horses to blow their savings on, the wealthy citizens of the Dutch Republic literally had more money than they knew what to do with. Local investments were limited and difficult to trade. Henry Hope, a banker rumored to be the richest man in Europe at the time, estimated that wealthy Amsterdam residents—his clientele—saved as much as 25% or more of their annual income.[3]

All these guilders looking for a place to go apparently spurred the entrepreneurial imagination of Abraham van Ketwich, an Amsterdam-based broker who became the father of the first mutual fund, Eendragt Maakt Magt, in 1774. The name wasn't exactly original; it was Dutch for the Republic's motto: "Unity Creates Strength."[4] Technically, Eendragt Maakt Magt wasn't exactly a mutual fund, but a trust. Consistent with its catchy feel-good name, it promised well-heeled investors the global diversification and richer returns previously accessible to only the mega-wealthy. Now, van Ketwich promised, you could invest with the big boys, the smart money, the high rollers of Amsterdam finance! Now you too could own a small stake in an exclusive collection of exotic securities from around the world! Van Ketwich also promised investors lower risk and higher returns than they could get at home. Why settle for 3% when you could be earning... 4%?

Amazingly, that was the basic pitch: the fund's portfolio was expected to generate 8% per year in dividends, with about 4% paid out to investors. The other 4% was used to buy back shares at random through a peculiar lottery feature. The fund invested in a diversified portfolio of Danish and Viennese bank loans, the postal services of Saxony and Peatlands, Spanish canals, Danish tolls, and Russian and Swedish government bonds.[5] The prospectus promised that these investments would be stored in an iron chest "with three differently working locks."[6]

Eendragt Maakt Magt was a winner right out of the gate, spawning at least two follow-on funds, Concordia Res Parvae Crescunt ("With Harmony Small Things Grow"),[7] and Voordeelig en Voorsigtig ("Profitable and Prudent"). But eight years later, the funds hit an air pocket when the Dutch made a game-changing error by backing the wrong horse: supplying the rebels in the American Revolution. The British were not amused. They blockaded the Dutch ports, snuffing out their global trading supremacy like a cigarette butt in a Heineken. Not only did this disrupt trade, it caused a banking crisis.

Eendragt Maakt Magt's buyback lottery was halted in 1782, and those attractive dividends reduced a few years later.[8] After losing 25% of their value at one point, the shares rallied back and the trust was ultimately liquidated in 1824 after fifty years of probably more excitement than investors had bargained for.[9]

While his clients may have been surprised by their rocky ride, van Ketwich himself had seen similar investments go bad before. A commodity price crash in 1771 had caused many New World plantations to default, resulting in some investors losing three-quarters of their capital.[10] The previous generation had been burned by the bursting of the South Sea Bubble. In every era there are safer, simpler, but less-sexy investments available, yet investors continue to prefer the exotic and complex, adding not only to excitement, but often also to expense. According to modern investment sage David Swensen, "As a general rule of thumb, the more complexity that exists in a Wall Street creation, the faster and farther investors should run."[11]

Back in the 1920s and '30s, most US investment funds offered investors little more than delusional pipe dreams. The Investment Act of 1940 lists abuses common at the time, from simple fraud to self-dealing, misleading promotional literature, usurious fees, bogus accounting, even outright looting. One victim was Charles Kettering, VP and Research Director at General Motors Corporation and, in the words of an SEC commissioner, "one of our most useful and finest citizens."[12] Kettering entrusted his savings to an investment fund, believing it was similar to life insurance or a savings account at a bank. The fund turned his $260,000 into $20,000.

Not all investment companies were run by crooks, however. Boston-based Massachusetts Investors Trust (MIT) wasn't cut from the same sharkskin cloth as those Wall Street funds. Founder Edward Leffler was a Milwaukee native with an evangelical passion for sales who had worked his way up from selling *Saturday Evening Post* subscriptions door-to-door to selling securities.[13] Longing for a product he truly believed in, Leffler created a low-cost diversified fund overseen by trustees who promised to put the clients' interests first. Just a plain and simple stock fund, with none of the leverage, creative pricing, and carnival excitement of Wall Street.

Initially, the fund held forty-five stocks, including household names such as AT&T, General Electric, General Motors, Kodak, and the B&O Railroad of Monopoly fame. Share prices at the time were high, close to $130 on average. A single share of one holding, Boston Insurance Company, sold for more than $680. For individuals, attempting to replicate the fund on their own was impossibly expensive. Given the steep trading costs of that era, copycatting this collection would cost around $6,600 at a time when the average American household income was around $3,500.[14]

Even for the affluent, managing a do-it-yourself equity portfolio was a formidable challenge. Today you can buy and sell investments, compute returns, and boast about your results anywhere, anytime with just a cell phone and a Wi-Fi connection. Doing it yourself was unthinkable in 1924: not only were costs high, but information was much harder to come by, a situation that didn't change until fairly recently. When I started in the industry in the early '90s, annual reports arrived by snail mail, many weeks after publication. Stocks were physical certificates delivered by courier, and independent research often meant a trip to the library.

By the time I left, I had a daily firehose of data, including hundreds of emails, conference call transcripts, investor presentations, and the latest financial reports for every public company in North America and beyond. My Bloomberg subscription brought real-time stock prices and an endless 24-hour news feed right to my desktop. All these new resources spectacularly increased my access to information, but threatened to drown me in a constant flood of facts and opinions.

My summer with Riley offered a bucolic sabbatical, although one with its own unique health risks. Every week or so one of my stablemates had an accident—a broken wrist, a separated shoulder, a kick in the face. I wondered when my own luck would run out. The beginning of the end came one sweltering August afternoon, when I suddenly lost my bearings and couldn't comprehend even the simplest instructions. While the coach yelled "Left! Go left! MAKE HIM GO LEFT!"

I somehow couldn't remember where left was, or how to get there. Decked out in my equestrian finery—leather boots, a tailored jacket, and a helmet that looked like a bowling ball with a brim—I was so baking hot, my brain had begun to poach.

Exiting the show ring, I fell to the ground. A paramedic rushed over in a golf cart. I lay on a picnic table babbling while the adults debated whether to send me to the hospital. We placed third or fourth, I've forgotten which, but I do remember the prize money: $400, the only money I made that summer, and a pittance against the amount I spent to be there. Of course, heatstroke and all, it was my best summer ever.

After that first attack—and as the paramedic had warned me—heatstroke became a recurring theme. My damaged elbow developed such vicious tendonitis I sometimes couldn't sleep. Physically I couldn't keep up with Riley, and financially, well, if wishes were horses, we'd all be broke. When my lease expired in December I didn't renew. But I had no regrets. Just photographs and memories. And two file folders full of barn bills. How lucky I was, to paraphrase Winnie-the-Pooh, to have had something that made saying goodbye so hard.

I said goodbye, with many carrots and gourmet horse treats. Riley went on to greater glory with a younger, braver woman, and I returned to life in the big city.

2

Small Is Beautiful

I'M SITTING IN Canoe, a restaurant fifty-four stories above Toronto, wondering if I'll recognize the man I'm meeting. I've checked out his mug shot online. White male; short, dark hair. That describes about 90% of North American financial executives, and probably 90% of the customers here as well. Looking around, I realize I'm the only woman sitting down; all the others are serving drinks. I relax. He doesn't need to know what I look like to pick me out in this crowd. The waitresses are half my age or younger and none of them is wearing a suit.

Canoe is as Canadian as a hockey-playing beaver who says "sorry" when you step on his tail. Actually, Bucky Beaver might be on the menu here. Canoe takes Canadian cuisine to new heights, offering milk-fed piglets from Quebec, chicken-fried sweetbreads, toasted bulrush brioche, and Algonquin grits. I've lived in Canada all my life and have never heard of any of these.

My man arrives a few minutes later. We're meeting to discuss a potential job opportunity: an underperforming fund that needs a new manager. Turns out the sick fund invests primarily in Canadian smaller companies—small caps—unlike my old fund, small-cap-focused but investing primarily in American stocks. For me, this is a deal-breaker. My US investment universe comprised almost 5,000 potential investments; the Canadian one, fewer than 300. This is the difference between shopping in Manhattan or Moose Jaw.

As a place to live, Canada has always been my first choice. But the country's stock market, the Toronto Stock Exchange—the TSX—is dominated by two sectors: financials (primarily banks and insurance companies) and energy. At the end of May 2018, these two groups made up more than half of the total value of the S&P/TSX Composite, the equivalent of the S&P 500. In contrast, real estate accounted for around 3% and health care only 1%.

Canadian financial companies are known for their high quality. In 2015, the country's banking system was ranked the soundest in the world by the World Economic Forum for the eighth year in a row.[1] These stocks are often described as *blue chips*, although the term originally referred to stocks with high prices, not high quality—blue chips represent the biggest bets in a poker game.[2]

"Blue chip" is in fact a meaningless term, suggesting a seal of approval that doesn't exist. Stocks can go from blue chip to bankruptcy the same way celebrities go from A-list to *Where Are They Now?* Yet many investors do prefer to stick with larger, better-known companies. Small stocks are perceived as lower quality, even when the underlying businesses are growing, profitable, and well-financed. Psychologists call this *familiarity bias*, the human tendency to prefer things we know, even if they are less attractive to an objective observer. Starbucks, for instance, feels like an old friend, even before we've seen her financial statements. International Rectifier, on the other hand, sounds more like a cyborg superhero, a name you may feel less comfortable seeing in your portfolio.

To me, preferring the most popular stocks makes about as much sense as going to a mall on Black Friday, competing in a crowded marketplace for picked-over merchandise. True bargains are harder to come by. And preferring large to small may also be a mistake; research has shown that large stocks tend to underperform smaller ones on average. One reason is that high growth rates are easier to sustain when you start small. In the words of UK money manager Jim Slater, "Elephants don't gallop."

Furthermore, size is no proxy for safety. Any stock can go to zero. One of the most compelling illustrations of this is a 2000 *Fortune* magazine story "10 Stocks to Last the Decade." Reporter David Rynecki surveyed "some of the top stock pickers in the country" and constructed what he called "a buy-and-forget portfolio." For long-term investors, wrote Rynecki, "these ten should put your retirement account in good stead and protect you from those recurring nightmares about the stocks that got away." His portfolio, made up entirely of widely-held large caps, went on to lose more than 30% of its value over the next ten years.[3] If you bought it, you'd be lucky if you *could* forget it.

Only one stock went up, Genentech, which almost tripled in price, while the other nine declined on average more than 50%. The stocks were Broadcom, Charles Schwab, Enron, Genentech, Morgan Stanley, Nokia, Oracle, Univision, Viacom, and my hometown favourite, Nortel, once so large it dominated the Canadian stock market. So while some dismiss the entire small-cap category as excessively risky, the real issue is whether or not any particular stock is a good investment. The big-cap bias benefits those of us who believe small is beautiful, with fewer competitors bargain hunting on our stretch of the savannah.

For me, small caps were love at first sight. My first job in the financial industry was at a firm that focused on discovering relatively unknown fast-growing smaller companies. Every morning we'd scour the earnings reports in the newspaper for obscure companies showing sudden increases in growth, then interview their leaders to determine whether this was a one-time blip or a long-term investment opportunity. The strategy was astonishingly effective and my first clue that common sense and independent thinking were better bets than running with the herd.

When I changed jobs in 1997, my new boss warned me that my love of small caps limited my career options. He advised me that small-cap jobs were fewer in number, and the largest funds and largest salaries were in large caps. After a couple of years helping him run one of the largest funds in Canada, however, I was thrilled when a small-cap position opened up.

That love is blind is a cliché for good reason: research shows we all tend to ignore information we disagree with, so-called *confirmation bias*. While financial types pride themselves on their objectivity and analytical rigor, the fact is, we're all human and need to constantly guard against being swayed by subconscious biases and strong emotions.

For example, regardless of nationality, most investors are irrationally patriotic, suffering from *home bias*.[4] Canadians, for instance, tend to own mostly Canadian stocks—which account for only about 3% of the total value of global stock markets—despite the ease with which investors today can take advantage of opportunities anywhere in the world. Similarly, one study found that German business students were more optimistic about German stocks than US ones, while at the same time American business students held the opposite view.[5]

Even professional investors are swayed by emotion. When one psychoanalyst took a random walk down Wall Street in 2007, he found more melodrama than you'll see on most reality TV shows. In 2007, UK psychoanalyst David Tuckett teamed up with Richard Taffler, a professor of finance and accounting at the University of Warwick, to explore how money managers make decisions. They interviewed fifty-two subjects in the US, Asia, France, and the UK. Most of their subjects had a decade or more of experience and personal responsibility for at least US$1 billion.[6]

In their first few interviews, the researchers were surprised to discover a massive disconnect between theory and reality.[7] Rather than being data-driven, objective, rational decision makers, the money managers appeared to be hopeless romantics, falling in and out of love with their investments. One manager, an accountant by training, described his infatuation with a stock referred to as Fast Foods, babbling on to embarrassing lengths about their restaurants, customers, and new products. He sheepishly admitted to sometimes visiting on weekends or on his way to work.[8] When asked to describe investments that did not work out, managers told stories of relationships gone awry, tales of betrayal, bad luck, and deep disappointment.

Taking credit for our successes and writing off mistakes to bad luck is human nature. Untangling luck from skill is the focus of Michael Mauboussin's book *The Success Equation*. Mauboussin, a Wall Street investment strategist, describes the varying importance of luck and skill in different activities. You can't outrun an Olympic sprinter by luck alone. Luck helps, but it's not enough. Winning the lottery is all luck and no skill, while winning at blackjack depends on a blend of both. Superior talent is obvious in activities such as rowing, basketball, and chess. Where skill is harder to judge—gambling and investing, for example—disentangling luck from skill is much trickier.

With more than 8,000 US mutual funds to choose from and 3,000 or so in Canada, separating the skillful from the merely lucky is like looking for diamonds in a mountain of cubic zirconia. Many experts now argue that the safest route is to simply invest in the overall market through *index funds* (funds that buy a representative basket of stocks that move in sync with the market), known as "passive" investing. With the advantage of significantly lower costs and maximum simplicity, the popularity of index funds has soared. From 2004 to 2016, money in index mutual funds grew nearly fivefold, to $2.6 trillion, approaching 20% of US mutual fund industry assets.[9]

While passions run high on both sides of this debate, one of the bibles of the passive faithful is *A Random Walk Down Wall Street*, a bestseller for more than forty years. Author Burton Malkiel argues that a blindfolded dart-tossing monkey can beat most "active" money managers; that is, traditional stock pickers like me. Exhibit A on the other side of this argument is Warren Buffett, probably the most successful investor of all time. His first investment fund, Buffett Partnership, grew on average just under 30% a year over its twelve-year existence, compared to the Dow Jones Industrial Average's relatively anemic 7%.[10] From 1965 to the end of 2013, the *book value* of his company Berkshire Hathaway (the value of the company's assets recorded on its financial statements) grew about 20% per year compared to the S&P 500's 10%.[11] While that may sound like Buffett's slowing down, bear in mind Berkshire Hathaway is now among the largest public companies in the world, so growing at a gallop is more challenging.

Some say Buffett just got lucky. In 1984, he refuted that argument by profiling a group he referred to as the "Superinvestors of Graham-and-Doddsville." Buffett's mentor was Benjamin Graham, a Columbia Business School professor and co-author with David Dodd of *Security Analysis*, probably the best-selling finance textbook of all time. The nine "superinvestors"—including both Buffett and his partner Charlie Munger—were all disciples of Graham. At the time of this talk, they had, on average, achieved triple the growth of the overall stock market for long periods of time. The secret to their success, Buffett explained, hadn't been a secret since 1934, when *Security Analysis* was first published. Anyone who read the book could have copied their investment strategy. Yet few other investors followed this approach, now known as *value investing*. "There seems to be some perverse human characteristic that likes to make easy things difficult," Buffett concluded. "Ships will sail around the world but the Flat Earth Society will prevail."

Buffett-worship is endemic in the investment industry, with both pros and amateurs reciting his well-known one-liners like articles of faith: "Price is what you pay; value is what you get"; "Our favorite holding period is forever"; "Be greedy when others are fearful"; and so on. Comments made at the annual meetings of Berkshire Hathaway become raw material for vast numbers of quarterly blurbs, blogs, and media stories. And every year 35,000 or so time-constrained Warren Buffett wannabees make the pilgrimage to Berkshire Hathaway's annual meeting in Omaha. Yet in my experience most investors are non-observant members of this particular religion. As Bill Maher said of Jesus Christ: "Was there ever a greater victim of name-dropping?"

Some believe Buffett wouldn't be Buffett if he started out today. In a 1998 *Financial Analysts Journal* article, "Where, Oh Where, are the .400 Hitters of Yesteryear?" investment guru Peter Bernstein argues that just as the superstars of baseball no longer achieve .400 batting averages, investors now and in the future are unlikely to ever again achieve the impressive track records of Buffett's superinvestors. Bernstein was inspired by the work of Stephen Jay Gould, a Harvard paleontologist and popular science writer. Gould believed that declining batting averages result from increased competition. As both batters and pitchers improve their performance, hits become increasingly harder to come by. As a result, no baseball player has achieved a batting average of .400 for a full season since Ted Williams in 1941. Bernstein was struck by how well Gould's explanation fit the investment industry, where the spread between the best and the worst had been narrowing for years, and the next generation of Warren Buffetts was nowhere to be found. For investors, writes Bernstein, "It's tough to outsmart a market in which so many people have become just as smart as you."[12]

The competition is fierce and grows fiercer all the time. Increasing numbers of math and computer experts have joined the ranks of traditional security analysts in the quest for performance. Yet rarely do most amateur investors factor this into their thinking. In his book *What Investors Really Want*, Meir Statman describes the error many do-it-yourselfers make, believing that investing is like hitting a tennis ball against a wall. Practicing against a wall, you can watch the ball and move into position to return it. In the stock market, you're competing with a mercenary army of well-educated, highly compensated professionals, the equivalent of taking on the top players at Wimbledon—all at the same time.

Statman recounts a conversation with an amateur investor planning to buy Japanese yen, believing the yen was poised to "zoom."[13] "Think for a moment," he explained. "You are on one side of the net, thinking that the yen will go up. Your opponent is on the other side, thinking that it will go down. One of you must be the slow one. Have you considered the possibility that the yen seller might be Goldman Sachs, Barclays, Bank of Tokyo-Mitsubishi UFJ, or another of many traders in the yen market who have offices in both Tokyo and New York and know more about both the Japanese and American economies than you can learn from your morning's *Wall Street Journal*?"[14]

For every buyer there has to be a seller, a guy who disagrees with you so strongly he's willing to take the other side of your bet. Outsmarting the pros is possible, but unlikely if you're trading on TV tips, Internet advice, or plain wild-ass guesses. Economist Fischer Black defined this as "noise trading... trading on noise as if it were information. People who trade on noise are willing to trade even though from an objective point of view they would be better off not trading. Perhaps they think the noise they are trading on is information. Or perhaps they just like to trade."[15] Of course, just as "that idiot driver!" is always the other guy or gal—never me or you—no one self-identifies as a noise trader.

Overestimating our own intelligence often leads us to believe we can predict the future, especially when it comes to the stock market. Market forecasting is a billion-dollar industry and an evergreen source of material for the financial media. Yet major market events are almost always surprises. In fact, unimagined—even unimaginable—events show up regularly in life, especially in the stock market. *Black swan*, a term popularized by Nassim Taleb's 2007 book, has become a cliché in the investment industry, replacing *perfect storm* as the favorite face-saver when reality refuses to comply with the experts' predictions.

To Europeans, black swans were once a figure of speech, like pink elephants and pigs that fly.[16] The irony lost its punch, however, when Dutch explorer Willem de Vlamingh arrived in Australia in 1696 and discovered what the locals already knew: black swans are as real as roast beef, and just as tasty.[17]

Taleb defines a black swan event as dramatic in consequence, virtually impossible to predict, but also inevitable. Despite all our efforts to predict the future, the disasters we expect—Y2K computer glitches, for example—don't materialize. Instead, we get 9/11, the bankruptcy of Iceland, or a powerful clique of greedy bankers knocking the global financial system to its knees.

Part of the problem, according to some, is that the financial industry is hunting for swans with outdated weapons. Taleb, for instance, dedicated his book to Benoit Mandelbrot, father of chaos theory and inventor of fractal geometry. In 2005, the two co-authored a column in *Fortune* magazine warning readers to ignore the risk metrics "spewed out by the pseudoscience of finance: standard deviation, the Sharpe ratio, variance, correlation, alpha, value at risk, even the Black–Scholes option-pricing model."[18] Mumbo jumbo to some, this is blasphemy to financial types.

Mandelbrot wasn't just trash-talking Wall Street; he arrived at these views through empirical research. As a scientist at IBM in 1961, he was invited to speak at Harvard University about his work on income distribution. He chanced upon a drawing on a professor's blackboard that looked exactly like his own data. Wondering at the coincidence, he was told this was, in fact, a graph of cotton prices. Prevailing theory predicted price changes that looked like a series of coin tosses. But the data didn't look like that. Using IBM's computers, Mandelbrot ran his own numbers. He discovered a distinct pattern. But not the one any economist would expect.[19]

"Far from being well-behaved and normal as the standard theory then predicted, cotton prices jumped wildly around. Their variance, rather than holding steady as expected, gyrated a hundred-fold and never settled to a constant value. In the world of financial theory, that was a bombshell."[20] Mandelbrot's ideas were soundly booed by the establishment: "The noise from academia was loud. Who was this Mandelbrot fellow, a grimy industrial scientist with a degree in applied mathematics, to challenge the elaborate models of the economics elite?"[21]

For his doctoral thesis, one of Mandelbrot's students, Eugene Fama, analyzed prices of the top thirty stocks in the Dow Jones Industrial Average. A similar pattern emerged: "Large changes, of more than five standard deviations from the average, happened two thousand times more often than expected. Under [conventional] Gaussian rules, you should have encountered such drama only once every seven thousand years; in fact, the data showed, it happened once every three or four years."[22] While Fama went on to win the 2013 Nobel Memorial Prize in Economic Sciences for his subsequent achievements, at the time, his fellow economists were unimpressed. For them, Gaussian rules were gospel. (*Gaussian* refers to so-called normal distribution, data that plots as a bell curve.) And since reality didn't fit their model, they ignored it.

According to spiritual teacher Byron Katie, when we argue with reality, reality wins—but only 100% of the time. Bad math, not mother nature, was a prime suspect in multi-billion-dollar screwups like the crash of 1987, the 1998 implosion of Long-Term Capital Management, and the 2008 financial crisis. Economist Mark Rubinstein has pointed out that for anyone who believes in the foundational theories of modern finance, the 20% market decline on October 19, 1987 had a probability of 10^{-160}. In other words, you shouldn't expect this event to occur even once in the estimated duration of this universe—20 billion years—or even in 20 billion reincarnations of it.[23] Or in layman's terms, it was damned near impossible.

Finance professor and quantitative investor Emanuel Derman has accused finance of *physics envy*: describing the world as if markets were governed by Newtonian-style laws when in fact, financial models are rarely more precise than metaphors. "In physics you're playing against God, and He doesn't change His laws very often. In finance you're playing against God's creatures, agents who value assets based on their ephemeral opinions."[24]

Physical properties like gravity are predictable; markets are not. Or at least not yet. The distinctive patterns Mandelbrot discovered can be found in both natural and human-made phenomena, complex systems including earthquakes, forest fires, heart rates, and financial markets. This discovery offered new hope for investors seeking to beat the market with complicated high-speed computer algorithms. One group, the Prediction

Company of Santa Fe, New Mexico, has been working on this since 1991. Their chance of success was estimated by Eugene Fama as "not zero, but close to it."[25] The company has been sold twice, first to mega-bank UBS and later to asset manager Millennium Partners.[26] Although no performance data are disclosed, it seems unlikely UBS would sell a goose laying golden eggs, so maybe the folks in Santa Fe still have a few bugs to work out.

While potential employers may be more impressed by graduate degrees in math, business, or computer science, my journalism background turned out to be a competitive advantage, arming me with interviewing and research skills as well as an almost pathological desire to question authority. Hired by a man who not only admired Warren Buffett, but actually followed his advice, I had the best possible mentor. We invested the old-fashioned way: studying businesses, analyzing financial statements, and deciding if stock prices represented bargains or not. In the words of Buffett: simple—but not easy. Day after day, I mined an imposing mountain of annual reports, 10Ks, 10Qs, proxy circulars, conference call transcripts, industry research, articles from database searches—every possible scrap of information that might help me ask better questions, build better financial models, and make better investment decisions.

While most mutual funds own dozens of securities, mine held only around twenty-five. Like Buffett, I believed in putting all my eggs in just a few baskets, and then watching them like a hawk. My goal was to invest in a handful of high-quality growing businesses. Most made everyday products like locks and keys, gas detectors, water filters—profitable, established businesses without the dice-rolling excitement of gold mines and oil wells.

By 2013, however, small caps were looking expensive. Many stocks on my radar screen were trading at prices 30 to 40 times their earnings per share. Compared to the long-term price-to-earnings ratio of the S&P 500—around 16—they looked obscenely expensive. When stocks trade at 40 times earnings, the folks who own them clearly have high expectations. Any whiff of disappointment can cause prices to collapse. One common explanation when a stock price takes a swan dive is that the company's earnings "failed to meet expectations." In truth, investor expectations failed to recognize reality.

When I lost my job that spring, the timing was perfect. Stock prices were soaring into the stratosphere, making bargains increasingly harder to find. My fund had a stellar track record, due to some combination of luck and skill. And horse show season was just a few weeks away. Sitting in Canoe, sipping my ginger ale and scoping out the skyline, I was looking forward to a summer sabbatical. In any case, my host wasn't jumping to make me an offer. After meeting me in person, he worried that I wouldn't fit in at his firm. "Your fund is odd," he said as we parted, "and you are weird. But before you do anything, call me."

Weird as charged, I took this as the highest compliment. I'd been flattered by the invitation, but it was too soon to rejoin the rat race. I wasn't sure where I was headed, but I wanted to leave my options open, wander aimlessly for a while. As former Buddhist monk Stephen Batchelor once wrote, "The problem with certainty is that it is static; it can do little but endlessly reassert itself. Uncertainty, by contrast, is full of unknowns, possibilities, and risks."[27] As an investor, I'd prided myself on being risk-averse. But perhaps that wasn't the wisest approach to life.

3

Creatures of the Casino

WHEN VICTOR NIEDERHOFFER won his first bet at the age of eleven—the same year he won the New York City eighteen-and-under tennis championship—his policeman father warned him "All gamblers die broke and most of them turn into degenerates along the way."[1]

Niederhoffer learned plenty about gambling and human nature as a kid growing up in Brighton Beach, New York, "the underdog capital of the world."[2] Then, after earning a PhD in economics from the University of Chicago, he excelled as a money manager. In 1996, he was named the number one hedge fund manager in the world, with a blistering hot fourteen-year track record: up 32% a year.[3] By October 1997, however, his fund was in tatters, wiped out by trouble in Thailand, where he'd invested on the eve of an economic crisis, compounded by a historic mini-crash back at home.[4] With his six daughters' tuition to pay, Niederhoffer was forced to mortgage his Connecticut mansion to survive and start over.

While he became "a Wall Street pariah, the butt of black humor and gossip," Niederhoffer had never claimed to be anything but a speculator.[5] Unlike most of us, he didn't blame bad luck, a perfect storm, or a black swan. Instead, he took full responsibility, attributing his fall to his own inflated ego: "I was only ranked number two. I wanted to be number one."[6]

Climbing back to the top took Niederhoffer almost ten years. In 2005, his Matador Fund gained 56%, more than ten times the market return. Two years later, however, Matador was in liquidation, fatally gored by 75% losses. Clearly, volatility works both ways; a stock that goes up like a feather in a funnel cloud usually goes down like a *Toontown* grand piano. Strategies that generate extraordinary gains are often the most likely to suffer extraordinary losses.

In fact, an investor who hits home runs year after year, never suffering a strikeout, is just plain suspicious. One famous money manager attracted the skepticism of his peers by posting positive results relentlessly for almost two decades, until he was finally arrested in December 2008. At age 71, Bernie Madoff was sentenced to 150 years in prison. Seven years earlier, in 2001, journalist Michael Ocrant had interviewed more than a dozen industry insiders, none of whom would go on record, but all of whom questioned the results Madoff was claiming.[7]

Unlike fraudsters and amateur speculators, Niederhoffer trades on proprietary empirically-based computer models—cold, hard data. Yet he likens speculation to sex: "Both are all-absorbing. And both have an air of the shameful about them: primal urges, evidently, drive people to do things they would not speak of."[8] But unlike most investors, he takes steps to thwart his own human instincts. One example, a story Niederhoffer tells in his autobiography, is the day his gold position was up $22 million. Worried he'd refuse to sell if the price headed south, he left instructions with his assistant to sell half his position if a price decline wiped out half his winnings. Ordering her to ignore him if he called with a change of plans, he went to Staten Island to play racquetball. When the price tanked, call he did, begging her to hold on, now convinced the price would bounce back. His assistant refused, saving her boss from financial ruin. (She later became his second wife.[9])

Few investors enjoy the same level of self-awareness. "We shall say quite a bit about the psychology of investors," wrote Benjamin Graham in 1949, in the introduction to *The Intelligent Investor*. "For indeed, the investor's chief problem—and even his worst enemy—is likely to be himself." Buffett describes Graham, his mentor, former employer, and friend, as "the greatest teacher in the history of finance," and *The Intelligent Investor* as by far the best book about investing ever written.[10] "To invest successfully over a lifetime does not require a stratospheric IQ, unusual business insights, or inside information," wrote Buffett in his preface to the 1973 edition. "What's needed is a sound intellectual framework for making decisions and the ability to keep emotions from corroding that framework."[11]

Known as the dean of Wall Street, Ben Graham was mentor to all of Buffett's superinvestors.[12] His Columbia University course, Advanced Security Analysis, spread the gospel of value investing for twenty-six years, attracting both serious students and seekers of stock tips—Graham was known for illustrating his lectures with real-time examples.

A spectacular student himself, Graham had earned his university degree at Columbia in only two and half years while working almost full time. When he graduated, he was offered positions in the Philosophy, Mathematics, and English departments. He later attributed his success as an investor to his intellectual discipline. Fortuitously, his arrival on Wall Street came at a time when investors were focused primarily on bonds. Stocks were considered "a near relative of the gambling casino." Even as publicly-traded companies grew more respectable, the Wall Street establishment eschewed Graham's empirical approach: "It seemed silly to pore over dry statistics when the determiners of price changes were thought to be an entirely different set of factors,"—namely emotions and inside information.[13]

As a result, factual information was largely ignored, except by Graham, a student of almost everything. His hobbies included translating Latin into Greek, writing sonnets and plays—one was produced on Broadway—and inventing a new type of slide rule.[14] For Graham, true investing requires that each security be thoroughly analyzed for its prospects for safety of principal and an attractive return. Anything else is speculation.[15] The distinction is clear in theory, but in practice, we're still inclined to view ourselves as investors, even when we're taking tips from CNBC. Regardless of our intelligence, human beings tend to be blind to our own shortcomings.

When psychologists Justin Kruger and David Dunning asked people to rate their own performance on tests of humor, grammar, and logic, they discovered that even the worst performers in every category considered themselves above average. In their paper "Unskilled and Unaware of It," they report that, except for the very best, almost everyone had an overly optimistic view of their own skills. (The elite performers were the only group who scored higher than their own expectations, mistakenly believing their peers were more competent than they actually were.) This creates a sort of catch-22 for the incompetent: "Not only do they reach erroneous conclusions and make unfortunate choices, but their incompetence robs them of the ability to realize it."[16]

Ben Graham almost didn't make it to Columbia University, believing he'd been outclassed by his peers. When he was turned down for a prestigious scholarship after acing the exam, he figured he'd failed the interview. He knew he'd scored points by talking about his favorite book, *History of the Decline and Fall of the Roman Empire*, so he blamed his failure on his weakness of character—masturbation specifically—convincing himself that the interviewer had somehow "detected this secret deformity of my soul and awarded my scholarship to someone purer and better than myself."[17] In this curious two-dimensional example of the Kruger-Dunning effect, Graham, a self-described prude, mistakenly rated himself above-average in perversion while underestimating his exceptional skills as a scholar.[18] Graham reapplied for admission the following year, discovering that his problem was bureaucratic rather than autoerotic; he'd actually won but the university had mixed him up with his cousin Louis, who was already attending Columbia on the same scholarship. Fortunately for Graham, for Columbia University, and for generations of investors, the mistake was discovered and he was offered full tuition and an apology.[19]

In his memoirs Graham describes himself as a dreamer and a poet, forced by financial circumstances to seek a more lucrative line of work. Despite his romanticism, he emphasizes taking an unemotional, empirical approach to investing. "It is easy for us to tell you not to speculate; the hard thing will be for you to follow this advice. Let us repeat what we said at the outset: If you want to speculate do so with your eyes open, knowing that you will probably lose money in the end."[20] Like his student Warren Buffett, Graham's wisdom is more often preached than practiced. He joked that his famous textbook had been "read by more people and disregarded by more people than any other I know." Speaking at a conference in 1973, Graham was questioned by one money manager who admitted he couldn't tell the difference between an investor and a speculator. Graham's patient response? "That's the sickness of the time."[21] He died three years later, decades before the sickness went viral, with 24-hour financial TV, trading apps, email tip sheets, and various other new pathogens encouraging would-be investors to become stock market thrill-seekers.

Traditional economists view human beings as rational decision makers, folks who do the math before making well-reasoned choices. Behavioral economists take a more realistic approach. Meir Statman, a pioneer in the field, describes behavioral finance as "finance with normal people." Normal people value utility, but we also care about expressive and emotional benefits. Almost any car can get you where you want to go, but vehicles often serve an additional role, as media for self-expression. An environmentalist may prefer a Prius, for example, while a soccer mom may dream of a monstrous Mercedes with seven seats, four-wheel drive, and a surround-sound entertainment system. Cars can also provide emotional benefits. One study found that 25% of Americans would consider buying a "midlife crisis" car to soothe the pain of middle age. Men preferred sleek, sexy sports cars like Corvettes and Mustangs, while women favored rugged, powerful SUVs.[22]

Investing, too, is often about more than just making money, with expressive and emotional rewards of its own. A survey of more than 1,200 US investment clubs found that almost all of them—96%—would have been better off simply investing in the overall market, through an index fund. By *not* picking stocks, they would have on average improved their profits by more than 25%. Yet many members found the experience enriching in other ways. Women spoke of education and empowerment; men talked about male bonding.[23] If we're truly more interested in making money than making friends, Buffett himself recommends index funds. With no special training or talent, anyone can succeed. "By periodically investing in an index fund... the know-nothing investor can actually outperform most investment professionals."[24]

John "Jack" Bogle has described all "active" investors as "creatures of the casino," trading shares back and forth with each other in a zero-sum game when they could simply invest in the overall market through a low-cost index fund. "You own American business, and you hold it forever."[25] Bogle has his own biases, of course, as founder of Vanguard, the first index fund company, in 1976. By 2018, Vanguard was managing more than $5 trillion for more than twenty million customers worldwide.

Clearly emotions have a huge influence over our behavior. While Graham worried that masturbation would keep him out of college in 1910, almost a hundred years later, in 2001, University of California professor Dan Ariely paid students at Berkeley $10 a session to masturbate for research. "We chose to study decision making under sexual arousal—not because we had kinky predilections ourselves, but because understanding the impact of arousal on behavior might help society grapple with some of its most difficult problems, such as teen pregnancy and the spread of HIV-AIDS," Ariely explains in *Predictably Irrational.*[26] The students answered a series of questions ranging from their commitment to safe sex to their probability of committing date rape. ("Are women's shoes erotic?... Would you find it exciting to spank your sexual partner?... Would you take a date to a fancy restaurant to increase your chance of having sex with her?..."[27]) The same questions were asked—with the help of a Saran-wrapped Apple iBook—when the students were aroused.

The results showed major differences in the students' decision-making in "hot" and "cold" states: excited students were nearly twice as likely to predict they would desire to engage in odd sexual activities, more than twice as likely to predict they would desire to engage in immoral activities, and 25% more likely to predict they wouldn't use condoms. Ariely's research partner, George Loewenstein, has described this effect as the *hot-cold empathy gap*, our failure to recognize how desire drives our behavior, for example, when a dieter loses resolve at the sight of the dessert cart, or a problem drinker tries to stop at just one drink. "Similar problems affect those who have problems with smoking, a failure to exercise, excessive borrowing, and insufficient savings," write Richard Thaler and Cass Sunstein in *Nudge: Improving Decisions about Health, Wealth, and Happiness*. The authors describe self-control problems as conflicts between our inner planners—the aspects of ourselves most like *Star Trek*'s logic-driven Mr. Spock—and our inner doers, our emotional, irrational inner Homer Simpsons.[28]

Like it or not, human beings are by nature creatures of the casino, more Homer Simpson than Mr. Spock. Our blindness to our own biases, shortcomings, and misconceptions prevents us from seeing the self-destructiveness of our own behavior. The closer we get to Spock it seems the closer we get to Buffett. Simply by trading less, for instance, most of us could improve our investment results. But for many of us, the urge to trade is too hard to resist. As Buffett himself has observed, "The stock market serves as a relocation center at which money is moved from the active to the patient."[29]

As a fund manager, I was never an active trader. But after years of watching prices flash on my computer screen all day long, an endless flow of "news," and mountains of documents to digest, my brain never stopped buzzing, dozens of data points demanding my attention all at once. The harder I worked, the less I got done. My doctor diagnosed me with Attention Deficit Disorder and prescribed amphetamines to help me concentrate. But to me, speed was the problem, not the answer. And true ADD is a lifelong condition, not a disease developed in middle age. I took the drugs briefly, but my heart wasn't in it. So I decided to try meditation instead.

4

Taming My Monkey Mind

AFTER RUSHING HOME and changing clothes, I drive off into the dark, headed for Starbucks. Between work and my mindfulness class, I need some caffeine to keep me going. It's January 2012, and I've signed up for an eight-week course at my local community center, Mindfulness-Based Stress Reduction.

Finding a course that suited my schedule, my budget, and my ambivalence had been a challenge. My doctor's downtown clinic offered a program catering to stressed out businessfolk, but the investment of time and money was substantial. I was looking for a quick fix, preferably one that was cheap and convenient. The community center, a five-minute drive from my home, fit the bill.

That first night, after the usual introductions, the instructor warned us that anyone with a history of abuse, trauma, addiction, or mental illness should proceed with caution. Stop, she said, if you experience any significant emotional discomfort.

At the time, I mistook this for an attempt to create mystique, suggesting we might potentially experience altered states of consciousness when all we'd signed up for was a basic introduction to the latest lifestyle trend.

Mindfulness-Based Stress Reduction, MBSR, was invented by Jon Kabat-Zinn almost forty years ago at the University of Massachusetts Medical School. Today it's probably the best-known and most-studied mindfulness program. MBSR has helped people suffering from medical conditions including cancer, chronic pain, and psoriasis, as well as psychological conditions such as anxiety, depression, and panic attacks.

Typically, MBSR comprises a rigorous eight-week program with one full-day retreat. Participants are encouraged to meditate for forty-five minutes a day or more, to establish the habit and start experiencing the benefits. This was more meditation than I had in mind. The community center's version was more my speed: less like boot camp, more like a spa sampler, with five-minute guided meditations, body scans, and pep talks on how to establish a regular practice.

The instructor stressed her connection with Kabat-Zinn, and the proven benefits of meditation. Even so, I remained skeptical. Plus, it was winter in Toronto and the community center shut the heat off after 5 p.m. By the time our class began two hours later, the gym felt like a walk-in freezer. Aside from the dramatic disclaimer, my main memory of the course is my struggle to keep warm. Each week, by the end of class, most of us had put on our winter coats and hats. Somehow the instructor either failed to notice or chose not to. Whether the topic of spirituality ever came up, I don't remember, distracted as I was by my struggle with hypothermia.

One of MBSR's selling points is its secular nature. While it evolved from Kabat-Zinn's background in Buddhism, MBSR is designed to offer the benefits of meditation to people of all faiths, making it welcome in most schools, hospitals, and businesses. Yet Stephen Batchelor has described the mainstream mindfulness movement as a Trojan horse: "Although doctors and therapists who employ mindfulness in a medical setting deliberately avoid any reference to Buddhism, you do not have to be a rocket scientist to figure out where it comes from." Mindfulness, says Batchelor, opens the door to other Buddhist values.[1]

Probably the most common challenge for newcomers to meditation is sticking with it; joining a group was recommended, to help us sustain our motivation. At our final class, the instructor provided a list of local meditation centers: a Zen temple, a group run by a Buddhist psychoanalyst, one focused on LGBT folks, and others. Ignoring any consideration of their respective traditions, I checked out each group's website and chose the one with the lowest cost (free) and most convenient location. I wasn't seeking enlightenment; just a Band-Aid for my burned-out brain.

The group I chose was right on the subway line and offered regular open houses. I dropped by one Tuesday evening, met with an instructor, and learned a technique called *shamatha*. Sanskrit for "peaceful abiding," this is the basic technique for all the Tibetan Buddhist traditions I'm familiar with, and other traditions as well. Initially, I had no interest in Buddhism, however, Tibetan or otherwise. I was there only to learn how to make meditation a daily habit. So at the end of my initial session, when the instructor gave me a cheat sheet and invited me back, I doubted I'd ever return.

Somehow I managed to commit ten minutes a day to sitting on my cushion, often spending most of the session wondering if I was wasting my time. Despite this meager effort, after a while, the sandstorm of data started to settle in my brain. And despite my initial indifference, I found myself signing up for various courses and retreats. My reading list gradually shifted from business to Buddhism. Then after I lost my job, I started volunteering at the meditation center. While still a workaholic, I was now applying my energy to helping with the website, serving tea and cookies, and, like a junkie offering free samples, even giving instruction.

Monkey mind is a metaphor helpful for explaining meditation to beginners: the mind that jumps from thought to thought, grasping one thing after another, from grocery lists to vacation plans, problems at work, past conversations, and on and on. Chasing a monkey through the jungle only makes it run faster and screech louder. If you sit quietly and wait patiently, your monkey is more likely to settle down. If you've never really examined it closely, watching your mind in meditation may give you a new appreciation for just how frenetic that monkey really is.

Practicing shamatha meditation trains your monkey mind, bringing it gently back whenever it wanders—again and again and again. At retreats, you may be doing this for twelve hours a day or more. Your feet might fall asleep, your back might ache, and you might question why you didn't choose a more relaxing way to spend your spare time. If you stick with it, however, you'll almost certainly see benefits. Over time, thoughts become less compelling. Strong emotions start losing their charge. By paying close attention to our own minds, we begin to see our habitual patterns and can develop the ability to see situations more clearly, unclouded by emotion, bias, memory, and other mental monkey business. "The whole idea of meditation," wrote Tibetan meditation master Chögyam Trungpa, "is to develop what is called the 'wisdom eye,' *prajnaparamita*, transcendental knowledge."[2] This process may take a lifetime or more, so believing in rebirth is helpful.

Few of us will achieve omniscience, but along the way, most of us fall into the trap of overestimating the clarity of our insight. Trungpa wrote a whole book about *spiritual materialism*—using spiritual practice to boost our egos instead of helping us see through our mental confusion. Decades before Kruger and Dunning wrote about how blind we are to our own incompetence, Trungpa spoke about *cocoon*, the web of mental habits and beliefs we use to construct our own personal versions of reality, blocking out things we don't want to see. Not only do we fail to accurately assess our own skills and shortcomings, but we harbor stubborn subconscious personal prejudices that can be harmful to ourselves and others. As neuroscientists have recently shown, we believe news and information we agree with and discount or ignore anything that challenges our worldview.

Journalist Kathryn Schulz wrote a book about being wrong—not the feeling of *discovering* that you've been wrong, but before that. She describes this as the feeling Wile E. Coyote experiences when he runs off a cliff in a Road Runner cartoon, just before he looks down. "Literally in his case and figuratively in yours," writes Schulz in *Being Wrong: Adventures in the Margin of Error*, "you are already in trouble when you feel like you're still on solid ground." Astonishingly, being wrong feels exactly like being right.[3] We keep running in the same direction, unaware the very ground we stand on is illusory. When we start seeing through our own delusions, much of what we thought was true about ourselves and the world may look quite different. "The bad news," writes Trungpa, "is that you're falling through the air, nothing to hang on to, no parachute. The good news is, there's no ground."

Learning to observe our own minds through meditation can create the distance we need to see ourselves and our experience more objectively. We may not always be pleased with what we see, but we'll probably be less susceptible to the Kruger–Dunning effect. And more open to seeing things as they actually are, rather than how we wish them to be.

Open-mindedness and objective analysis are hallmarks of Buddhism. Back in the fifth or sixth century BCE, the Buddha himself told his followers to question his every word, to test his teachings out for themselves, "Just as a goldsmith would test his gold by burning, cutting, and rubbing it, so you must examine my words and accept them, but not merely out of reverence for me."[4] And while some Buddhists argue their tradition is science, not religion, many Buddhist teachers now and in the past have been trained as monks and nuns. Tibet was unique in its enthusiasm for this lifestyle; when the Chinese invaded the country in 1959, almost a quarter of the male population were monks. Presumably, they viewed themselves as religious practitioners rather than scientists.

The most revered Tibetan Buddhist teachers are *tülkus*, reborn masters from previous generations. When a great teacher dies, he (few are women) typically leaves clues to help identify his successor. Trungpa, for instance, was discovered as an infant in a remote part of Tibet. After escaping the country as teenager by trekking through the Himalayas and leading hundreds of others to safety, he brought Tibetan Buddhism to America, founded Naropa University, and wrote so many books his translation team is still working on them thirty years after his death. Scientists may not recognize him as a reborn spiritual superstar from the past, but Trungpa's great accomplishments suggest he was more than just a lucky pick.

The scientific support for meditation is a hot topic among modern meditators, including Tenzin Gyatso, the fourteenth Dalai Lama, who in 1987 began meeting with scientists to discuss the intersection of meditation with developments in clinical science. These dialogues later led to the founding of the Mind and Life Institute, a nonprofit organization committed to supporting further investigation into the nature and inner workings of the human mind, using both contemplative and clinical methods.

Whether you regard Buddhism as science, religion, or just another flavor of self-help, the core ideas are intriguing. Impermanence, for instance, the idea that nothing lasts forever, is difficult to argue with. Our thoughts are more transitory than the weather. Even buildings crumble to dust if you wait long enough. We all age and die, but it's unpleasant to think about so most of us live our lives as if we're the exception to this rule.

Financial planners routinely question clients about their life insurance coverage, estate planning, and similar reminders of mortality. Asking questions is an essential part of the job, but some believe the most important ones don't get asked. In 1983, George Kinder formulated three questions that laid the ground for a new style of financial planning:

1. If you had all the money you needed, what would you change about your life?
2. If you have only five to ten years to live, how would you change your life?
3. If you had just twenty-four hours to live, what would you consider was missing from the life you've lived?

These three questions prompted serious soul-searching, waking people up to their true priorities, enabling them to redirect their time and money toward what mattered most to them.

Kinder, as a young accountant, saw his work preparing tax returns as merely a way to finance his passions for literature and Buddhism. But over time, his spiritual beliefs became a competitive advantage. "I needed to make tax work human by knowing my clients as fellow human beings," he wrote. "Remarkably, I soon discovered that knowing my clients well turned up countless deductions and credits that a more superficial approach would never have revealed."[5] Later, he became a financial planner, after clients sought advice on bogus tax shelters they'd been sold by unscrupulous financial advisors.

Kinder now coaches other planners, offering seminars, online programs, and certifications through the Kinder Institute of Life Planning. He's written a number of books and won awards for his work and leadership in the industry. A dynamic public speaker, Kinder shares compelling examples of clients who've changed their lives for the better in response to his three questions. In his keynote address for the 2011 New Model Adviser Conference, Kinder tells the story of one client, a workaholic who felt trapped by his business responsibilities. His work left little time for his wife and three young daughters. After working with Kinder to better align his life with his priorities, the client called one day from the road. He was living his dream, biking across America. Kinder recalls his words: "George, I just wanted to let you know, if I were to die tomorrow, I've accomplished everything that I wanted in life. My life is rich with meaning and I'm truly fulfilled." A year or so later the man died in his early fifties of a brain tumor.

For Kinder's clients, contemplating their own deaths becomes a wake-up call to start living their lives, a strategy borrowed from a traditional Buddhist practice called *the four reminders*, shorthand for "the four reminders that turn your mind to the *dharma*," or the Buddha's teachings. The first reminder is to contemplate our precious human birth, our good fortune of being born both human and "free and well-favored," meaning we have food, shelter, and the freedom—from political freedom to just plain free time—to study and practice meditation, which from a Buddhist perspective, is the path to peace.

The second reminder is impermanence—"the life of beings is like a bubble" and "death comes without warning." The third reminds us to carefully examine the impact of our actions—karma—on ourselves and others. (*Karma* literally means "action" rather than fate.) And the fourth reminder is the certainty of death; never to forget that eventually every one of us will be separated from our homes, friends, and possessions. Not exactly the core marketing messages of the modern mindfulness movement.

Mindfulness has become the Silly Putty of self-help, taking on the shape and color of whatever domain it's dumped into—education, psychotherapy, sports, sex, parenting, food, the military, addiction recovery, and more. Yet despite the positive press, meditation is not for everyone. Just like investing, the rewards of meditation are not without risk. In both cases, the rewards get most of the media and all of the marketing budget. If disclosed at all, the risks are often buried in the fine print. In theory, peacefully abiding with your thoughts sounds relaxing, but we're not always thrilled by what we find when we peek into the corners of our minds. We all have thoughts we block for good reason, ugly truths and painful memories. Meditation can open your eyes to more than you bargained for. As Chögyam Trungpa noted, "Meditation is not a sedative; it's a laxative."

Not only do the various risk factors cited by my MBSR instructor affect a quarter of the North American population or more, even people with no history of addiction, trauma, or mental illness can hit frightening potholes along the path. Unlike many, I'd been warned at my first meditation class to proceed with caution. But I wasn't listening. I remembered it only two years later, at a weekend retreat, when I hit some turbulence myself, a brain-melting afternoon of abject terror. Stunned by my newfound capacity to scare myself senseless, I went to a psychologist, literally for a sanity check. (I passed.) Then I started reading the research.

Willoughby Britton is the leading expert on what she now calls "Varieties of Contemplative Experience," formerly known as "The Dark Night Project." Britton is an assistant professor at the Brown University Medical School, with a PhD in neuroscience and many years' experience practicing and studying meditation in both Asia and North America. She's published numerous papers on the benefits of mindfulness for everyone from pot smokers to cardiac patients. But in 2012, when she presented her research findings to the Dalai Lama, she focused on the risks rather than the rewards.

Britton had interviewed more than sixty experienced meditation teachers, Buddhist scholars, and practitioners—including some of the rock stars of the mindfulness community—seeking data on difficulties they'd experienced. Not "difficulties" finding a comfortable cushion or the perfect posture, but clinical impairment: the inability to work or take care of children for at least one month. Subjects told her that disturbing experiences were common and considered normal. One told Britton, "if you go far enough in your spiritual practice, this is going to happen. It's part of the path."[6] More alarming, the meditators' difficulties had lasted, on average, more than three years, with a range of three months to more than a decade.

People reported experiencing the world as not solid. Objects flickered. They couldn't tell if they were awake or dreaming. Some felt like they'd been struck by lightning or plugged into an electrical outlet. Emotions could go into overdrive, sometimes flooding people with feelings of euphoria, but more commonly with terror. Many suffered what Britton terms "de-repression of psychological material... a volcano of memories and traumas that seems to pour out of the meditator but without much control."[7] Many of these people had been meditating for years with no problem. Then, typically, the trouble started on a retreat and afterwards seeped into their everyday lives. Those who sought medical help received diagnoses like bipolar disorder and schizophrenia.

Despite these unadvertised side effects, mindfulness has become the drug of choice for North American corporations eager to reduce health-care costs and improve employee engagement. Insurance company Aetna, for example, reported saving $2,000 per employee on health-care costs, with a $3,000 per-person increase in productivity.[8] But if corporate wellness programs trigger tsunamis of trauma that land employees in psych wards, the folks in HR may have some explaining to do. Historically, meditation is a tool for seeing clearly, yet it seems the modern mindfulness industry is stubbornly ignoring growing evidence that meditation has a downside. It's all fun and games, it seems, until somebody loses an I.

Not only are the risks ignored, the rewards are often overstated. One of the most well-known and prolific researchers in the field is Richard "Richie" Davidson, founder of the Center for Healthy Minds at the University of Wisconsin. He reviewed the state of meditation research in his 2017 book, *Altered Traits: Science Reveals How Meditation Changes our Mind, Brain, and Body*, co-authored with his friend, best-selling author and fellow psychologist Daniel Goleman. The book provides a history of mindfulness research, which Davidson and Goleman have been part of since the late 1970s, both personally and professionally. They describe the strengths and weaknesses of the research backing the claims made for meditation, arguing that many studies don't stand up to academic rigor. The primary benefits that *have* been proven through well-designed research include better attention, less reactivity to emotional stress, prosocial behavior, and improved compassion.

Probably the largest review of meditation research to date is a 2014 meta-study in *JAMA Internal Medicine*, a publication of the American Medical Association. A team of researchers analyzed more than 18,000 published studies, systematically evaluating the quality of their research and the strength of their findings. Fewer than fifty of the papers met their criteria, and the conclusions were positive but lukewarm: "Mindfulness meditation programs... show small improvements in anxiety, depression, and pain with moderate evidence and small improvements in stress/distress and the mental health component of health-related quality of life." The benefits were similar to the use of antidepressants.[9]

While no scientist has yet evaluated the effectiveness of meditation on investment performance, in 2016, the CFA Institute, the professional body for financial analysts and money managers, launched its own initiative. After a survey revealed a high level of interest in meditation among members, Jason Voss, a lifelong meditator and the organization's content director, spent three years researching and creating on online course, The Meditation Guide for Investment Professionals. Because the institute isn't ready to go full-lotus into the mindfulness business, the program provides an overview of the benefits of meditation for investment professionals, plus a 20% discount on membership in eMindful, a web-based service offering instruction and support.

Like most corporate efforts, the CFA Institute's program targets gains in on-the-job performance rather than spiritual awakening, with goals including reduced stress, improved mental focus, and overcoming behavioral biases. Yet the investment community seems to remain blind to the deeper potential of meditation—tapping into natural intelligence, that *wisdom eye* Chögyam Trungpa wrote about. Neuroscientists, psychologists, meditation practitioners, and others have all started collaborating to better understand the opportunity presented by the natural intelligence of human beings, says Voss. "But the investment community for whatever reason has ignored that conversation," he continues, "I think because they see it as squishy and not quantitative."

When I started meditating, my fund's performance was leading its category. So if mindfulness had any positive impact, I couldn't tell. But personally, I soon felt less frazzled by the flashing lights and the daily deluge of data. Also, I became more aware that Lady Luck was my co-pilot—as much as I wanted to take full credit for my fund's performance.

Over time, my karma ran over my dogma; my actions started speaking louder than my words. After I left the industry, I still talked about the thrill of hunting for cheap stocks, but I gradually lost interest in annual reports and financial ratios. I put most of my savings into low-cost index funds. In the past, I'd spent all my waking hours researching investment ideas. Now I was open to accepting whatever returns the stock market might offer. Meditation turned out to be a more powerful tool for personal productivity than I bargained for: I stopped stock picking and started living my life as if I might actually die someday.

5

The Fruit Flies of Finance

WESLEY "WES" GRAY didn't need a Buddhist financial planner to make him look death in the eye. He spent four years in the US Marine Corps, including a stint in Iraq embedded in the Iraqi army. Late one night, he and a friend idly calculated their odds of surviving. Estimating 180 convoy trips, 40 combat missions, plus 30 miscellaneous potentially fatal encounters, they calculated they might face as many as 500 hundred chances to die before heading home.[1]

Gray learned how to speak Arabic, but the cultural barriers to communicating with the Iraqis proved much steeper than the linguistic ones. Marines prize teamwork and leadership by example. The Iraqi military leaders saw themselves as kings, their soldiers as their servants. The marines' assignment was to train the local army, but the two forces had little in common. Motivation was part of the problem. The marines were fighting for honor and pride in their country; the Iraqis, for money, around $4,000 a year, pay that was often late or missing in action. One *jundi* (Arabic for soldier) told Gray the enemy paid better, offering a thousand-dollar bounty for killing an American. He claimed to know a sniper in Baghdad with "a garage full of BMWs and stacks of cash."[2]

Gray's military service was an unconventional detour from the "intellectual waterboarding" of the University of Chicago's PhD program, an environment he's described as "sweatshop meets international math competition." He'd been planning to sign up for years, and the timing was never quite right. Emails from a buddy at boot camp inspired him to request special permission for a four-year sabbatical.

As a lifelong value investor, Gray had already braved one of the great cultural chasms of finance, earning his MBA at the University of Chicago, the birthplace of Efficient Markets Theory (EMT). For the efficient markets faithful, value investing is a waste of time. Gray's PhD faculty advisor was none other than the father of EMT himself, Eugene Fama, that former student of Benoit Mandelbrot who went on to win the Nobel Prize.

A high school sports star, Fama had majored in Romance languages at Tufts University, planning to become a high school teacher and sports coach. He didn't study economics until his junior year, but when he did, he found his calling.[3] "I was enthralled by the subject matter," he later explained, "and by the prospect of escaping lifetime starvation on the wages of a high school teacher."[4] At Tufts, Fama helped analyze stock market data for a professor's forecasting service, attempting to devise an effective method for predicting the future. But what worked for a small selection of stocks would always fail when applied to a broader sample, sparking Fama's curiosity.

In 1965, as a PhD candidate at the University of Chicago, Fama coined the term *efficient markets*, referring to the view that stock market prices reflect all available information, not instantly or perfectly, but effectively enough that stock picking is pointless and index funds are the only rational investment.[5] Fama's theory transformed the image of the stock market from a Wild West casino to a well-oiled machine that automatically adjusts prices in response to new information.

Given his earlier work at Tufts, Fama arrived at the University of Chicago at an especially fortuitous time. The year he began his MBA, 1960, brokerage firm Merrill Lynch made an initial grant to the university to establish the Center for Research in Securities Prices (CRSP). The goal was to create a database of stock prices going back to 1926. At the time, no one knew for sure how stocks had performed historically. Merrill Lynch wanted a conclusive answer to help convince consumers to invest. The database would also create a laboratory for future researchers to determine if stock prices followed patterns or demonstrated predictable relationships with other data such as economic indicators.

Expected to take six months and cost $50,000, the project lasted more than three years and ran up a tab around four times the original estimate. Working from published manuals of historical stock prices, students constructed a database from scratch. Early on, the project's leaders, Professors James Lorie and Lawrence Fisher, realized they needed to correct for both typos and inputting errors. A computer program was written to help hunt down bad data, searching for unlikely price jumps and impossible fractions. The researchers discovered that the category of "common stocks" included more than fifty different types of security. Dividends were taxed seven different ways. And they needed to account for thirty-nine different potential capital changes—events like stock splits, mergers, and reorganizations.

The answer to Merrill's question was that, after taxes and trading costs, the typical American investor would have earned

8% on average by investing in stocks, double the typical savings account rate or the yield on US government bonds, which had remained below 4% for decades.

After its launch in December 1963, Lorie worried that CRSP might lose its funding if the data went unused. He asked Fama for help, proposing a study of stock splits, events where companies divide their shares to reduce the price per share. (For instance, when Apple stock was trading for more than $645 in June 2014, the company split the shares seven-for-one, bringing the price per share down below $100.) In 1969, Fama and three colleagues, Fisher, Michael Jensen, and Richard Roll, were first to publish research based on CRSP data.

Like fruit flies for geneticists, the CRSP database has played a vital role in modern finance, providing the raw material for decades of research by students, economists, professional investors, and anyone else taking a scientific approach to the stock market.

"At this stage in our lives we've essentially memorized the CRSP/Compustat database," jokes Wes Gray, who today manages money with his partners at Alpha Architect in Broomall, Pennsylvania, far from the shark-infested waters of Wall Street. (The CRSP/Compustat data combines CRSP's historic stock prices with Compustat's details from companies' financial statements.) The partners boast of their "disdain for flash," proudly posting a photo on their website of the firm's "official roadshow vehicle," an eleven-year-old Honda Civic. Alpha Architect aspires to achieve active, affordable alpha for its clients by investing according to a "data-driven, evidence-based, systematic model." (*Alpha* refers to the value added by stock picking, the extra return you get over the market return, referred to as *beta*.)

After returning safely from Iraq, Gray had set out to finish his dissertation, arguing that value investing works. He built a database of nearly 4,000 stock picks from ValueInvestors Club.com, a popular website for idea-sharing by money managers and others. His conclusion? Club members were, in fact, more skilled than lucky, which he saw as proof of the value of value investing.

When he sent his advisor an early draft of his research, Gray received a chilling email that began, "Your conclusion must be false." He rushed to Fama's office. "Sweating profusely, with the prospect of the PhD title slowly slipping away, I asked one of the world's most famous financial economists for clarification." The problem, as it turned out, wasn't the data, but the conclusion. Fama reminded him that for every winning trade, there's a loser on the other side. So while Gray was correct in identifying the ValueInvestorsClub members as skilled, they were only a small sample of the total population of value investors. Since investing is a zero-sum game, whatever profits they'd racked up represented other investors' losses.

Value investing was a family tradition for Gray. Growing up on a ranch in the Rockies, near Eagle, Colorado, he raised animals and sold them at the country fair. To teach him to invest wisely, Gray's grandmother sent him a copy of Ben Graham's *The Intelligent Investor*. "I was twelve at the time and instead of being overwhelmingly appreciative, I was secretly depressed it wasn't a Nintendo. Nonetheless, I read the book and loved it. I was hooked on value investing."[6]

Graham was a fundamental investor, hunting for bargains by carefully studying financial statements and making mathematical calculations by hand. Since computers became widely available, increasing numbers of investors, referred to as *quants*, have taken a quantitative approach, often developing proprietary "black box" mathematical models that can be highly complex and at times unpredictable. Long-Term Capital Management's spectacular 1998 implosion was attributed to models that failed to realistically reflect human behavior. As journalist Roger Lowenstein wrote, "Long-Term Capital's partners were shocked that their trades, spanning multiple asset classes, crashed in unison. But markets aren't so random. In times of stress, the correlations rise. People in a panic sell stocks—all stocks."[7]

While Wes Gray is a quant, he believes in simplicity, poking fun at the disconnect between extreme mathematical complexity and common sense: "How does one risk-manage a machine-learning algorithm trading leveraged exotic derivatives with a jump-diffusion model infused with a touch of fractal mathematics and string theory?" His 2013 book *Quantitative Value,* co-authored with Tobias Carlisle, lays out his investment strategy in plain English. Reading Gray's book was an epiphany for me, a lifelong value investor, describing a model that dramatically increases stock-picking efficiency, lowers the cost, and at the same time eliminates behavioral bias. Strategy-wise, Gray and his team were targeting the same criteria I once did, managing money the way I might myself if I had a PhD from the University of Chicago. In simple terms, their quantitative value model eliminates companies that show signs of financial distress or questionable accounting. After screening for bargains, it ranks the winners on the strength of their long-term business fundamentals. The result is forty or so stocks the team believes are the best value investments available.

The team rarely tinkers with their model. The quantitative value strategy represents almost fifteen years of work. "We're always testing ideas and thinking hard about our process, but at some point, if it ain't broke, don't fix it," says Gray. They also don't override the model, adding or subtracting stock picks of their own. "We always look at the names and think, God that's stupid. Why would we ever own *that*?" But experience shows that *that* is where the value lies, beyond the limits of investors' comfort zones.

Taking a systematic approach to emotionally charged situations is a lesson learned in the Marine Corps. Standard Operating Procedures (SOPs) are evidence-based rules to live by when going with your gut can be fatal. In fact, rules-based models have been shown to outperform human forecasts in fields ranging from baseball to Bordeaux wine. Michael Lewis's book *Moneyball* told the story of how the Oakland Athletics outperformed the competition by building a team based on objective statistical data instead of conventional baseball wisdom. Similarly, Orley Ashenfelter, a Princeton University economist, built a weather-based model that proved a better predictor of future wine prices than human experts.[8]

Emotions create a huge handicap for human decision-makers. Fear and greed often get in the way of objectivity. Part of Warren Buffett's advantage may be his superhuman ability to stay the course at times like the period between June 30, 1998 and February 29, 2000, when he was down 44% while the market was *up* 32%. The financial media dubbed him "yesterday's man" and called for his retirement. As a self-employed multibillionaire, his lagging performance didn't threaten his job security. Yet few investors can stick with their strategy through such an extreme test of faith.[9]

Buffett laughs at the idea of market efficiency; he's said he'd be "a bum on the street with a tin cup" if markets were efficient. Other critics have taken a scientific approach, using the CRSP data to document various inefficiencies that undermine Efficient Markets Theory. Smaller stocks, for example, and stocks with low market prices relative to their book values (the value of the company's assets as recorded on its financial statements) are two categories where bargain-hunting investors have historically made money. Inefficiencies like these are referred to as *anomalies*, exceptions to a rule that exists only if you believe in efficient markets. "Most so-called anomalies... don't seem anomalous to me at all," wrote Fischer Black, a former University of Chicago professor. "They seem like nuggets from a gold mine, found by one of the thousands of miners all over the world."

Early on, consumers wishing to profit from the wisdom of the sages in Chicago had few options. Dimensional Fund Advisors (DFA) was the one of the few firms to offer quantitative money management to individual investors. The firm was founded in 1981 by David Booth and Rex Sinquefield, University of Chicago alumni. As a student, Booth found his first finance class daunting. But Professor Fama assured him the course would be the most practical one he'd ever take. If the folks in Stockholm awarded a prize for understatement, Fama would have won that too. Booth and Sinquefield were so convinced of the value of Fama's theories, they built their business around them. Starting with a small-cap fund, DFA expanded over time into other US and global equities, fixed income, and even socially responsible funds. By the end of 2017, the firm was managing $755 billion for individuals and institutions in twenty-five countries.

Initially Booth and Sinquefield sought institutional clients only, concerned about the impact of impatient individual investors.[10] Eventually, however, they relented, but advisors who wished to offer DFA funds to their clients have to first survive the company's rigorous screening process, then pay their own way to attend in-house training. Despite these hurdles, or perhaps because of them, in 2015, the firm topped the list of US fund firms most trusted by advisors.[11] And the University of Chicago's business school was renamed The Booth School in 2008 after a $300 million gift from David Booth, the largest in the university's history.

Like DFA, Wes Gray's firm at first focused on managing money for a smaller number of large clients, an easier way to keep the lights on than courting mainstream investors with a few thousand dollars each. Communicating clearly with a smaller number of clients is easier, too, reducing the risk that they panic when performance is down. But in 2014 Gray and his team launched its first exchange-traded fund, or ETF, offering their quantitative value strategy to all.

Exchange-traded funds were the brainchild of Nathan Most, head of new products at the American Stock Exchange, in the late 1980s. Trading volume was down and Most hoped a new product would restore its vitality. At the time, some investors were still mailing checks to mutual fund companies when they wanted to purchase units, making it impossible to know what price they'd pay. Additionally, then as now, prices for mutual funds were set at the end of each day, so orders placed in the morning were filled at end-of-day prices.

Most saw an opportunity for a competing product that traded on the exchange like a stock, with prices constantly updating. From his experience trading safflower seeds and coconut oil futures, he was familiar with warehouse receipts, which enable traders to avoid dealing in physical quantities of commodities such as orange juice, oats, or crude oil. He thought the same convention could be applied to securities, creating receipts for a basket of stocks. Investors could then buy or sell these receipts on the exchange like stocks, without postal delays or the risk of end-of-day price surprises. But to launch his invention, Most needed the blessing of the Securities and Exchange Commission (SEC).

While Most pleaded his case to the regulators, folks at the Toronto Stock Exchange (TSE) saw the potential for the same type of security in Canada to help win back investors scared away from stocks by the 1987 crash. The Ontario Securities

Commission, the local equivalent of the SEC, proved more open to the idea. Thus Toronto became the birthplace of the first exchange-traded fund, Toronto 35 Index Participation Units, or TIPs. A trust held shares of all the stocks in the Toronto 35 Index, then issued units based on the stocks' value. The price of the basket closely tracked the value of the stocks due to arbitrage, where short-term traders buy one and sell the other to profit from any price discrepancy.[12]

On March 9, 1990, the first issue of TIPs started trading, more than twelve million units worth $210 million.[13] One brokerage firm refused to participate, calling the units risky and unethical, a form of program trading, the computerized activity blamed for the 1987 crash.[14] Nevertheless, TIPs were so popular that the exchange issued more and more, with the total almost tripling by September. A year later, they were up to forty-two million and among the most actively traded issues on the exchange. One TSE executive described the demand as "insatiable."[15]

But the buyers were mainly institutions—mutual funds, pension funds, and other large investors—not individuals. Although journalists wrote enthusiastically about TIPs, consumers remained leery, and financial advisors had no incentive to promote them. For advisors, TIPs paid a commission of only 3%, compared to typical mutual fund commissions, called *loads*, of 4% to 9%, plus ongoing annual management fees. For investors, not only were the commissions on TIPs lower, but the annual expense ratio was probably the best investment bargain in history, an incredible 0%. Over time, the TSE raised the price to 0.04%, the equivalent of four cents for every $100 invested. Not surprisingly, the price didn't cover the costs, and the exchange ended up subsidizing the product by about $2 million a year. As a result, despite their indisputable popularity, TIPs were killed off in March 2000, just days short of their tenth birthday. Almost $6 billion worth of TIPs and its less-popular younger sibling HIPs—based on the TSE 100 index—were exchanged for units of a similar product called i60s, which tracked the performance of the new S&P/TSE 60 Index.

In January 1993, the first American ETF was launched, Standard & Poor's Depositary Receipts, SPDRs, tracking the S&P 500 index. The ticker symbol was SPY, but the nickname was "spiders." The exchange celebrated its new arrival by hanging a nine-foot inflatable spider over the trading floor.[16] Within ten years, SPDRs accounted for more than half of the trading volume on the American Stock Exchange.[17] By 2018, SPY had grown to gargantuan size, around $270 billion, and given birth to more than a hundred SPDR-branded progeny. Globally, more than 6,000 ETFs worth more than $4 *trillion* were investing in everything from the Dow Jones Industrial Index to Chinese A Shares, Build America Bonds, the Markit iBoxx USD Liquid Leveraged Loan Index, and a whole host of securities with embarrassingly cute tickers like MOO and VEGI for agricultural products, TAN for solar energy companies, and HACK for cyber security stocks.[18]

In addition to the advantages Most first recognized, many ETFs offer better tax efficiency than traditional mutual funds. In 2013, about half of equity funds in the US paid out capital gains, but only 4% of ETFs, and mostly in much smaller amounts.[19] ETFs have also been described as more democratic, allowing all investors access to once-exotic assets like gold bullion, currencies, and *alternatives*, which offer the hedge fund-style excitement of managed futures, merger arbitrage, and other arcane asset classes. The flipside of this democracy is that some investors buy products without fully understanding the risks.

Some ETFs are so volatile and poorly understood, consumer advocates have lobbied regulators to ban them. Inverse products, often with the word "bear" in their names, are bets that prices will fall, while leveraged products typically offer double ("2×") or triple ("3×") exposure, magnifying your gains or losses. For example, Direxion Daily Healthcare Bull 3× (CURE), moves up or down triple the one-day move of the health-care stocks in the S&P 500, while Direxion Daily Healthcare Bear 3× (SICK), moves in the opposite direction. Many consumers mistakenly view inverse ETFs as insurance against price declines, when these products are in fact designed for very short-term exposure, typically one day. As the ETF's price fluctuates, your investment can get eaten up by volatility. Unless you understand the math, stay away.

Sometimes even plain vanilla ETFs disappoint. They may have high tracking error, meaning there's a large gap between the ETF price and the value of the index it's meant to mimic. Some fail to attract enough assets to survive and are merged or closed down. Other potential pitfalls include sometimes-erratic pricing, usually at the start and finish of trading. To avoid buying or selling at unexpected prices, investors can use *limit* orders, specifying the maximum price they want to pay to buy an ETF or the minimum price at which they wish to sell. Also, some experts recommend avoiding the first and last fifteen minutes of the trading day, when prices are often most volatile.

Until 2008, all US ETFs were index funds, offering investors the ability to invest in baskets of stocks replicating specific indices such as the S&P500, Dow Jones 100, or "Qubes" (QQQ) on the Nasdaq-100. More recently, active ETFs have been launched as well. Similar to mutual funds, these ETFs hold stocks selected by money managers. For many years, all active and passive US ETFs and most Canadian ones were required to report their holdings daily. Thus, Alpha Architect's decision to offer their products as ETFs meant potential copycats could see every holding, every day. Yet Gray is confident most won't. For individual investors, an ETF is more tax-efficient than mimicking the portfolio on your own, not to mention the time and expense involved. Why bother, when you can, as Gray says, "just type in the ticker and have a nice day"?

Since the advent of active ETFs, various attempts have been made to build a better mousetrap for index investors, one that captures both alpha and beta. (Traditional index funds, because they're designed to track the overall market, by definition match the market return, or "beta.") Viewed as a middle ground between active and passive, these products have been wildly successful, accounting for more than $700 billion globally by mid-2017, with almost 90% of this money in US-listed exchange-traded products.[20] Called "smart beta," "strategic beta," "intelligent indexing," and similar self-congratulatory names, the category is marketing magic, making traditional index funds look downright dim-witted by comparison.

One of the key criticisms of index funds is that all the major indices are market-capitalization weighted. (*Market capitalization* is calculated by multiplying the stock price by the total number of shares outstanding.) So if Apple is 3% of the S&P 500, SPY would own 3% Apple. Critics argue that this means index funds systematically overinvest in the largest, most expensive stocks while at the same time underinvesting in the smallest, least expensive stocks. During the tech bubble, stocks like Cisco and Nortel skyrocketed in value, becoming larger and larger holdings in index funds as their prices grew increasingly disconnected from reality. When they eventually crashed back to earth, billions of dollars of investors' savings evaporated.

Some smart beta ETFs target exposure to specific factors such as size, value, or momentum, a strategy known as *factor investing*. Others feature alternative weighting schemes, rejigging an index to achieve a better balance of large and small, expensive and inexpensive. Still others are complex creatures straight out of Dr. Seuss, a whole zoo of factors rolled into one rare beast with a friendly face and a catchy name.

While factor investing may improve your performance, here again, patience is essential. No factor works all the time, and most are cyclical, underperforming sometimes for years at a stretch. In 2014, MSCI, an index data provider, reported that for the forty-year period beginning in 1975, all seven of the firm's proprietary factor indices outperformed the MSCI World Index. Yet each individual index underperformed for long stretches. The value-weighted index, for instance, underperformed for two consecutive years, the quality index for three, and minimum volatility for four.[21] Clearly, investors need unshakable confidence in their chosen strategy. If you can't stomach two or more consecutive years of underperformance, factor investing is not for you.

Alternative weighting may be a more suitable choice for investors with no strong conviction about any specific factor. The oldest strategy is equal weighting, investing in equal amounts of each stock, used by Wells Fargo to manage the first index fund in 1971. The fund was created by John "Mac" McQuown, a mechanical engineer and Harvard MBA, with the help of University of Chicago professors Fama, Lorie, and Fisher. They spent six years immersed in CRSP data building a model before testing it on their first live guinea pig, the six-million-dollar Samsonite Luggage Fund.

Investing equally in each of the 1,500 or so stocks on the New York Stock Exchange was efficient in theory but expensive in practice. Every price fluctuation threw the weights out of balance, requiring trading to reset the stocks to equal positions. With market-capitalization weighting, positions automatically increase or decrease as stocks go up and down. As a result, much less trading is required, making the funds easier and less expensive to manage. After a few years, Samsonite switched to market-capitalization weighting.[22]

Today, equal-weighted index funds are more feasible, but relatively unpopular. Probably the most common alternative weighting scheme is RAFI (Research Affiliates Fundamental Index) methodology. *Fundamental indexing* refers to indexing based on fundamental company characteristics like sales, cash flow, or dividends rather than the stock's market price. The long-term cost-benefit tradeoff for RAFI or any other smart beta product remains open to debate. Because these products typically cost more than so-called bulk beta—low-cost traditional index funds—not only do you need to believe a strategy works, but also that it's worth the extra cost.

Additionally, as the field becomes more crowded and the products more complicated, consumers face a growing risk of mistaking marketing hype for science. An award-winning 2015 paper by Denys Glushkov of the University of Pennsylvania's Wharton School asked the question: How smart are "smart beta" ETFs? Examining fifteen strategies, Glushkov identified dividend yield as the worst performer, *underperforming* its benchmark by almost 4% a year from 2003 to 2014.[23] In other words, investors who stuck with "stupid" traditional index-tracking products made the wiser choice. Overall, the study found no evidence that *any* of the strategies studied outperformed their benchmark indices. Additionally, most of the smart ETFs took a multifactor approach, sometimes accidentally combining factors that cancelled each other out.[24]

Not only do consumers often flock to products with shaky scientific support, but the definitions used to construct ETFs often stray significantly from the formulas used in research studies. For instance, while the traditional academic measure of value is low price-to-book-value, many smart beta ETFs use composite numbers made up of earnings yield, cash flow yield, forward price-to-earnings, and various other data points. *Quality* is an even more nebulous concept, including any combination of: earnings growth, profitability, accounting quality, return on equity, low leverage, and a laundry list of other items. While smart beta promises the low cost of passive, the alpha of active—half the calories but twice the caffeine—sometimes it looks more like Madison Avenue spin than University of Chicago research.

Furthermore, when Wall Street rewrites the tested recipes of academia, one of the new ingredients is often extra fees. One potential Wall Street sales partner praised Alpha Architect's products, but told Gray and his team the fees lacked sufficient "juice" to fuel his salesforce. Instead of charging investors extra to buy friends like these folks, the firm sells direct to keep costs low. Gray says that sales calls are almost 100% inbound; investors read his books or the Alpha Architect blog and they're sold.

The man-machine hybrid of quantitative investing has been compared to freestyle chess, an approach invented by grand master Garry Kasparov a year after his 1997 defeat by IBM's Deep Blue. Kasparov challenged Veselin Topalov, another world-class competitor, to a game where both players partnered with PCs that provided instant access to a database of millions of moves. He later wrote that the computers made mistakes almost impossible, but instead of reducing the importance of the humans' input, "the advantage still came down to creating a new idea at some point."[25]

"Having spent a lifetime analyzing the game of chess and comparing the capacity of computers to the capacity of the human brain," wrote Kasparov, "I've often wondered, where does our success come from? The answer is synthesis, the ability to combine creativity and calculation, art and science, into a whole that is much greater than the sum of its parts."[26]

The world's top-ranked chess player in 2015 was a down-to-earth Norwegian who has described computer chess as "like playing with someone who is extremely stupid but who beats you anyway."[27] Starting at age eight, Magnus Carlsen initially learned new strategies from books. Motivated by sibling rivalry—he has three sisters—Carlsen improved his game until he was top-ranked in the household. After he ran out of suitable opponents at school, Carlsen went online. Unlike many modern players, however, he prefers flesh-and-blood competitors. One writer attributed Carlsen's success to his unorthodox training. Once dubbed "the Mozart of chess," he plays a more creative game, talking about "harmony" and "poetry" rather than optimizing search algorithms.[28] A grand master at age thirteen and number one in the world six years later, Carlsen was also named one of the sexiest men of 2013 by *Cosmopolitan* magazine. On his twenty-fourth birthday, he challenged the entire population of Norway on live TV, with opponents participating via downloadable app. Carlsen checkmated them in fifteen moves.[29]

Just as Magnus Carlsen has gained a competitive advantage by relying on human creativity in a world obsessed with technology, advocates of behavioral finance are the current reigning champs of the market efficiency debate. Richard Thaler, one of the fathers of behavioral finance, won the Nobel Prize for economics in 2017. His work has influenced public policy in the US and other countries, where governments have designed programs in ways that attempt to take advantage of human behavior. Rather than advertising the benefits of reducing energy consumption, for example, utilities show high-use homeowners how their usage compares with their neighbors'. Whether they're embarrassed or just competitive, many respond by cutting back.[30]

While the behavioral finance folks appear to be in the lead, the debate isn't over. And the CRSP data is amazingly adaptable, used as ammunition by both sides. Despite the existence of anomalies, Fama and others view factors as additional betas (market returns) available in efficient markets, while his opponents consider these evidence of irrational investor behavior, reflecting predictable behavioral biases. The value factor, for instance, reflects investors' preference for large, well-known stocks, making bargains more common among less-popular smaller companies. The behavioral argument was articulated most succinctly in a fabled but unpublished paper by economist and former US Secretary of the Treasury Lawrence Summers that began "THERE ARE IDIOTS. Look around."[31]

Whether you agree with Summers or not, other studies have found that high-quality stocks tend to outperform low-quality ones, and low-volatility stocks outperform high-volatility ones—in other words, investors are rewarded for *not* taking risk. And research has found no discernable evidence that stock market fluctuations reflect the efficient incorporation of new information. The 2013 study "What Moves Stock Prices: Another Look" examined the history of major stock market moves, concluding that, "Only a minority of the fifty largest moves in the last 255 years can be tied to fundamental economic information." The same study did, however, lend support to Summers' IDIOTS hypothesis, finding that large moves on consecutive days tended to be in opposite directions, "as if investors significantly change their long-run views... only to change their minds again the next day."[32]

In stock markets, as in life, change is the only constant, and we must adapt to survive. Marines are taught that complacency kills; that "Victory leads to overconfidence, overconfidence leads to laziness, and laziness can lead to death."[33] So while Wes Gray and his partners rely on time-tested, data-driven, evidence-based models, they're always on the lookout for fresh ideas, the latest research, and new hypotheses to test.

In December 2015, Alpha Architect launched two new ETFs, QMOM for US quality momentum stocks and IMOM for international ones. While raised on value investing, Gray and his team spent enough time reading the research and reverse-engineering every momentum strategy they could find to grow convinced they needed to add this capability to their battle plan. Not only is momentum "the premier anomaly" according to Eugene Fama, but when value is in the dumps, momentum tends to shine.

The farther you get from Wall Street, it seems, the greater the willingness to admit that finance is not physics and there's plenty we still don't know. What Buddhists refer to as *don't-know mind* is rare in the financial industry, the willingness to remain curious and open to new possibilities even when you think you know the answer.

When I managed money, I was certain my way was the right way, that buying bargain small-cap stocks was the surest path to better performance. Other investors preach other religions, from following trends to following Twitter traffic. Yet like yin and yang, shadow and light, spectacle and audience, polar opposites are fundamentally interdependent. Both active and passive investors may argue the superiority of their approach, yet each depends on the other. Perfectly efficient markets would offer no reward for analyzing and trading stocks, but without the bargain hunting of active investors, markets would have no mechanism to become efficient, a conundrum known in finance as the Grossman–Stiglitz Paradox.

To a Buddhist, Grossman–Stiglitz isn't a paradox. Interdependence is a fundamental tenet. Nothing exists in a vacuum; the world is a complex web of relationships between people and things, all in constant flux. Venturing out of my comfort zone, I was starting to open my eyes to the full range of opportunities—value and momentum, active and passive, quantitative and qualitative, human and computer. Include everything. The wisdom of this approach was proven again as I followed the first skirmishes in the next big industry turf war—the Battle of the Robo-Advisors.

6

Do Androids Dream of Electronic Financial Advice?

GREEN AND PURPLE lights bounce off the weird white geometric background as 2,000 or so tech buffs stare out from the cavernous black conference hall. It's May 26, 2010 and on stage, Jon Stein looks like a contestant on a retro sci-fi game show. Seventy-eight thousand viewers have tuned in to watch his presentation online, but it's all those live human beings that are unnerving: not just the audience but the panel of judges, elite Silicon Valley technology gurus and venture capitalists Stein hopes will help him raise the money he needs to fuel his dream.[1] He has six minutes to convince them that his radical model for financial advice is a winner, that the last three years of his life haven't been a total waste of time.

Stein was up all night, fueled by caffeine and endorphins, obsessively typing last-minute ideas into his BlackBerry. His friends and co-creators Eli Broverman, Kiran Keshav, and Anthony Schrauth have all invested a year or so of their lives in Stein's vision, Betterment, and he can't let them down. Today is not only the project's public debut, but also launch day for its website, the first day real live customers can sign up.

Startup Battlefield is the main event at TechCrunch Disrupt New York 2010, a three-day festival of innovation with speakers from AOL, Google, Facebook, Yahoo!, plus a surprise appearance by New York City Mayor Michael Bloomberg, himself a tech billionaire. Like hippie squatters in a derelict mansion, crowds of cyber entrepreneurs and their followers roam Merrill Lynch's former data center, a massive 100,000-square-foot space in a gargantuan four-acre freight terminal in the West Village.

Charlie Merrill and Eddie Lynch were once, like Stein and his pals, upstart entrepreneurs taking on the banking establishment, "convinced that there was a wonderful opportunity for any business that would cut loose from obsolete methods on the one hand, and not attempt to profiteer on the public on the other."[2] Merrill Lynch prided itself on bringing Wall Street to Main Street, advertising to the public and demystifying investing. "We loved being the underdog and doing things others thought we couldn't accomplish," said Win Smith Jr. at the firm's final shareholders' meeting, following its purchase by Bank of America in 2008. "We were optimists who always knew we would get better and better and be number one in whatever we chose to pursue."[3]

For a few minutes on September 11, 2001, this fortress-like data center provided a safe haven for fleeing Merrill Lynch executives, but only briefly, before a gas leak was discovered.[4] Built in 1935 by the New York Central Railroad, the St. John's Park Terminal served the High Line, an elevated heavy freight line connecting Manhattan meatpacking plants and other industries to the outside world.[5] The floors are among the strongest in the city, built to withstand up to 100 fully-loaded freight cars at time, perfect for Merrill's giant mainframes, but overkill for this crowd with their featherweight laptops.

For Stein, winning six minutes in this green-and-purple limelight was a coup; from hundreds of entries from around the world, Startup Battlefield picked only twenty to pitch live on stage. Two more were chosen by the audience.[6] The prize is $50,000 and the Disrupt Cup, a sterling silver bowling trophy acquired and repurposed for this role.[7] But Stein's got much more at stake: he's walked away from a high-paying career, invested $640,000 and three years of his life, and convinced Broverman, Keshav, and Schrauth to join him.[8] On stage, he boasts of Betterment's status as a both a registered broker-dealer and a Registered Investment Advisor, with up to $500,000 insurance per account from Securities Investor Protection Corporation (SIPC). This single slide in his deck represents a momentous milestone, the finish line of a bureaucratic marathon convincing US financial authorities to trust Betterment with the public's money. "I thought, look, these are reasonable people and this is a good idea," Stein says later. "They're going to want to help make this happen. If we talk to them, they'll be on our side and they'll see that we're doing something right and good for customers." Instead of the three months he'd expected, winning over the regulators took two years.[9]

Fortunately, Stein's poker buddy and co-founder Broverman is a securities lawyer with the necessary mix of professional skills and entrepreneurial determination.[10] "Both Eli and I have a bit of a 'bring it on' mentality," says Stein. The thicker the complexity, the fiercer their determination to cut through the clutter. There's always a way, says Stein. Plus, it's fun to overcome challenges and defy expectations.

Facing TechCrunch's mob of digerati, venture capitalists, media, and online gawkers, Stein launches into his pitch. "Betterment is a replacement for your savings account," he says. "It's a simple idea that everyone should have a way to save intelligently." Just set the Betterment Speedometer to your preferred risk level, and software does the rest. A few clicks and your savings are invested in a sensible, low-cost, no-frills portfolio of stocks or treasury bonds, with an annual fee a fraction of what you'd pay for traditional investment advice.

Judge Chi-Hua Chien, a former partner with renowned venture capitalists Kleiner Perkins Caufield & Byers, says he's impressed by the simplicity. Chris Sacca, former Head of Special Initiatives at Google, private equity investor, and—his website says—once described by the *Wall Street Journal* as "possibly the most influential businessman in America,"[11] suggests the site lacks credibility, with none of the mess and bewilderment consumers expect from a financial website. Betterment, he says, looks too much like a toy. Stein, a former banking consultant, knows firsthand just how harmful and lucrative bewilderment can be. Betterment was funded from the proceeds of his former career, and actually inspired by it.

"That's how the old financial firms take advantage of people, by confusing them," he says. "The incentives of the old firms are to keep you confused, and that's how they make money." One bank he knows of built branches in low-income districts where customers were more likely to bounce checks. By charging $40 per bounce and promoting so-called free checking accounts, the bank succeeded in adding $160 on average per customer per month to its revenue line.[12]

In 2009, IBM's Institute for Business Value published a study of more than 2,700 investors, government officials, and investment company executives from around the world, concluding that that "for the past twenty years, the financial markets industry has profited by capitalizing on 'pockets of opacity'—i.e., creating, buying and selling complex products..."[13] While industry executives were prioritizing one-stop shopping, clients were seeking unbiased advice and excellent customer service. The study found that independent advisors and asset managers better understood their customers' needs than the global mega-banks, and were thus better able to serve them.[14] Furthermore, only 12% of industry executives considered their firms effective at capitalizing on new technology.[15] What better time in history to launch an agile, client-focused, technology-driven solution like Betterment?

If Betterment is a toy, so is an iPhone. It's hip, fun to use, and deceptively powerful. It's designed to be friendly, but not just superficially—the kind of friend who comes to dinner, cooks the food, washes the dishes, and helps your kid with his homework. Sort of like Investment Mary Poppins—but you don't need a dysfunctional family to sign up.

Input your age and income and choose a goal: safety net, retirement, or general investing. Transfer money in from your bank account (you can transfer out just as easily if you change your mind), and the software does the rest, divvying up your dollars between a dozen or so ETFs from low-cost providers like Vanguard and iShares. Over time, the software automatically rebalances the portfolio, so if your target is 40% bonds and your stocks soar into the stratosphere, Betterment will automatically sell down your stock exposure to get you back to that 40/60 split.

Early on, the financial media dubbed software-driven investment management companies *robo-advisors*, and the name stuck, despite its air of anti-cyborg slur. Cost-wise, robo-advisors look like a weapon of mass destruction for the financial advice industry, with prices as low as free for some services. At the beginning of 2018, Betterment offered two account types, charging 0.25%, "25 basis points" in industry-speak, for their basic, digital-only service, with no minimum balance; or 40 basis points (0.40%), for premium accounts, which provide access to Certified Financial Planners (CFPs) and other professionals for clients who invest $100,000 or more. This 0.25% or 0.40% compares to a fee of 1% to 2% for traditional advice from a broker or financial planner.

Whether you're working with a human or robo-advisor, the cost of the actual investments is typically extra, and can vary dramatically, depending on which ETFs, mutual funds, or other investments are recommended. Part of the value added by a service like Betterment is expertise in selecting the most efficient ETFs, ones that give you the best bang for your basis points. Betterment illustrates the cost comparison on its website, comparing its 70% stock IRA portfolio at 13 basis points to the 2016 ETF industry average cost of 52. Unlike Betterment, some robo-advisors are owned by fund companies or have other conflicts of interest that may result in higher costs or portfolios that include proprietary funds, which may or may not represent the best choice in each category. Some, unlike Betterment, also charge trading fees, fees for money transfers, fees for rebalancing, fees for mailing paper statements, and other fees. However, most disclose their pricing and fees clearly, so comparing costs is relatively easy.

One early criticism of Betterment was the argument that it was charging a fee for something investors could easily do themselves, as detailed advice on constructing a portfolio of low-cost ETFs is available for free online. Of course, theoretically, it's also easy to quit smoking (don't light up) or lose weight (eat less, exercise more). Reality is always much messier, especially in the world of finance. Not only must do-it-yourself investors wade through a tidal wave of complicated products, they need to understand tax rules, portfolio optimization, best execution, and other skills only a robot could love. "I could in theory fix my car myself," says Dan Egan. Betterment's Director of Behavioral Finance and Investing. "But I'd much rather have somebody who knows what they're doing and does it professionally do it for me."

Historically, that's been the role of human financial advisors, and initial media coverage of robo-advisors emphasized the man-versus-machine angle. Rather than waging war, however, Betterment wants to join forces: Betterment for Advisors was launched in 2014, a service that enables financial advisors to offer their own clients the same user-friendly Betterment platform and low-cost online services.

Behavioral coaching is a key benefit of one-on-one financial advice, helping clients sit tight when they're tempted to cave in to their own self-destructive impulses.[16] When markets tank, clients are more likely to panic, and benefit from a friendly phone call reminding them of their long-term goals. Until the robo-advisors survive a stress-test like 1987 or 2008, no one knows how steadfast their clients truly are. Initial reports suggest that machines, too, are prone to panic under pressure: when the Dow Jones Industrial Average had a historical one-day hiccup in February 2018, the websites of Betterment and a number of competitors crashed briefly, infuriating some clients and delighting their critics. Yet the problem wasn't isolated to robo-advisors; similar outages hit behemoths Vanguard, Charles Schwab, and TD Ameritrade. While critics assert that clients will rush for the exits without the hands-on intervention of a human advisor, in fact, many frustrated clients were trying to get *in* on the decline, not out.

At Betterment, "don't panic" is built into the software. From the very beginning, Stein designed the interface to help investors make better decisions, avoiding the video-game excitement of traditional brokerage websites. As an economics major at Harvard, Stein studied with Irven DeVore, one of the university's all-time most popular professors, famous for his course in Human Behavioral Biology, also known more simply as Sex. For more than thirty years, DeVore taught almost a third of Harvard undergraduates, enthralling them with tales of his life as an anthropologist—imitating mating buffaloes and describing the noisy orgasms of female chimpanzees. "I teach by humor and shock," DeVore told a *Boston Globe* interviewer in 1997. "There's no excuse for boring students when you're talking about human nature."[17]

The intersection of economics and human behavior fascinated Stein. Even before he started working in the industry, he wondered if there wasn't some way to help investors make wiser decisions. Traditional brokerage websites seemed to take advantage of predictable human failings to drive transactions, rather than encourage long-term buy-and-hold investing. Cyborg anthropologist Amber Case describes this as *panic architecture*, deliberately demanding our attention and fueling compulsive interaction. Websites like Facebook, for example, constantly remind us to check in and participate in the ongoing flood of chatter, reeling us in and holding our attention.[18]

By showing daily stock returns, brokerage websites fuel behavioral biases such as *myopic loss aversion*, where investors perceive stocks as riskier than they really are. "Investors who check their accounts every day will see losses about half the time by chance alone," says Dan Egan. "Not only that, but they show it to you in bright red or green, and that really does trigger a lot of emotional fight-or-flight-type responses." Because we feel losses more intensely than gains, we're likely to conclude that the market is excessively risky and reduce our exposure to stocks. While investors may believe daily returns are useful information, they're better off focusing on the long term, reducing the temptation to try to time the market.

Another driver of bad behavior is viewing individual security returns. This fuels a bias known as *correlation neglect*, where people look at each holding in isolation instead of considering their overall portfolio. We forget the rationale for owning a diversified portfolio—some investments will be up when others are down—and focus on each security's return individually. Watching daily ups and downs encourages trading, which more often than not hurts your long-term performance. Just as philosopher Lao-Tzu described governing a country, managing an investment portfolio is like frying a small fish: you destroy it with too much poking.[19]

Rather than turning investing into an exciting but expensive video game, Betterment emphasizes goals-based investing, boring, perhaps, but better for you. Customers target goals like saving for a house, education, an emergency fund, or retirement. An interactive graph illustrates the likelihood of achieving your goal based on the size of your account today and potential future market returns. If you're saving for your kid's college education ten years from now, for example, you can see right away if you're headed for a shortfall, providing a psychological nudge in the direction of scraping together a few more dollars today to increase your odds of meeting your goal in the future.

Over time, the sophistication of Betterment's website has evolved, with features such as Tax Impact Preview, which calculates the tax consequences of asset allocation changes before you commit to your decision. Customers who were informed that they were triggering taxes made 14% fewer allocation changes, and the larger the tax bill involved, the less likely they were to go ahead. Research has shown that most investors are unaware of the tax impact of transactions until they file their tax returns in April the following year. By showing the tax bite at the time of each decision, Betterment hopes to encourage wiser choices.

The team is constantly testing new ways of helping their clients be more successful investors. One startling discovery is that contacting clients in a downturn may actually encourage self-defeating behavior. Investors who have a set-it-and-forget-it outlook to begin with are more likely to take action if they receive an email informing them that the market is in a tailspin. However, clients who continually check and recheck their accounts are even more prone to pushing the panic button. They're primed for action and need support to sit tight. By sending targeted emails to hyperactive types only, Betterment avoids inadvertently upsetting the others.

The man-versus-machine press coverage in the early days of robo-advisors has died down as the synergies between the two grow more apparent. For investors interested in low-cost, professionally-managed investment portfolios, a Betterment-style solution is hard to beat, whether you deal with a robo-advisor or go through a traditional advisor. At the same time, in-depth financial planning represents money well spent for folks seeking personalized advice, especially if your financial situation is more complex. By embracing technology, advisors can offer a new breed of *cy-fi*—cyborg finance—human and machine each doing what they do best, making advice more affordable, more convenient, and more transparent.

In the sci-fi classic *Do Androids Dream of Electric Sheep?*, the basis for the movie *Blade Runner*, technology has developed to a state where the key distinction between humans and androids is empathy, one of the few human qualities software can't yet replicate. The protagonist, Rick Deckard, is a bounty hunter based in post–World War Terminus San Francisco. Searching for rogue androids, he administers the empathy-detecting Voigt–Kampff test. While human beings are expected to flinch at the mention of calfskin wallets, butterfly collections, or a recipe for boiled dog stuffed with rice, androids fail the test by responding slowly or insincerely, revealing their lack of genuine empathy.[20]

This was author Philip K. Dick's bleak vision of 1992, the far-distant future when he wrote *Androids* in 1968. Fortunately, humanity has avoided the global radioactive contamination Dick imagined, although we're at least twenty-five years behind his expectations for android technology.[21] We have robots for manufacturing, defusing explosives, and even vacuuming our homes, but none even aspires to empathy. For the foreseeable future, expecting an automated advisor to hold your hand through major life events like death or divorce is unrealistic. But for basic investment advice, they're pretty much indistinguishable from a well-informed, highly organized human being who watches your account 24/7 regardless of whether you have $10 or $10 million. They won't invite you to dinner, but you'll get an email right away if you're trading too much, or if you can add money to your account to avoid a taxable event.

While machines excel in areas of efficiency and accuracy, most human beings are way ahead of them when it comes to empathy and compassion. Yet from the start, Betterment aspired to more than technological excellence. Despite his background in finance, Stein's goals were never purely financial. "I didn't want to be a consultant making a ton of money and not really helping anyone."[22] Money, he says, doesn't correlate with happiness. He values good friends, family, and the opportunity to work at something he believes in. Banking for him was almost an apprenticeship, where he could learn the ropes, knowing all the while he wanted to run his own show. He'd picked out the name Betterment before he knew what the business would be, and rather than a brainstorm in the shower, it was the product of thousands of conversations with other people, including classmates at Columbia Business School, where he enrolled in 2007 to start building his dream.

As a Harvard economics major and CFA, Stein knew more than most about investing. While he was working as a bank consultant, he managed his own portfolio online in his spare time. He opened accounts at seven different brokerage firms but couldn't find a single website that offered all the tools he wanted in one place. In his day job, he'd learned to write code in Excel, discovering a knack for boiling down reams of data into easy-to-use decision-making dashboards for pricing mortgages or car loans. Managing money through seven different accounts was time-consuming and inefficient, so Stein wrote a program to consolidate his information: the prototype for Betterment. When he showed it to his friend Eli Broverman, Broverman wanted one too. After inquiring into Stein's business plan and discovering he could use some help on the regulatory side, Broverman joined as co-founder. In the age of the Internet, it seems, frustrated Ivy Leaguers are the brothers of invention.

Betterment aims to maximize your return on a market portfolio. While that sounds like an oxymoron—aiming for both average and above-average at the same time—in fact, assuming the fees are reasonable, almost any robo-advisor is probably a better choice than doing it yourself, with additional benefits such as greater tax-efficiency, automatic rebalancing, and ongoing research and analysis to make sure you own the most efficient ETFs in each category. Features like automated contributions and goals-based investing encourage better behavior that should also improve performance. But the greatest benefit investment-wise is probably the asset allocation, the work Betterment and others do to ensure your portfolio offers an optimal mix of stocks, bonds, and other asset classes based on your risk tolerance.

Asset allocation is an important driver of returns. Historically, stocks have outperformed everything else over the long run, yet most people are better served by a blend of stocks and bonds. Timing is everything and either one can offer more or less of a bargain at any given time. Bonds tend to hold their value better but offer lower returns, while stocks have more potential for upside, but also disappointment. The shorter your time horizon, the lower your tolerance for volatility, and therefore the lower the proportion of stocks you should hold. Most advisors recommend moving more of your money into less risky assets as you approach your investment goal—retirement for example, or your child's entry into college. This reduces your exposure to a major decline just when you need the money. Robo-advisors can do this automatically.

Poor diversification is a common pitfall for individual investors, who often overinvest in their favorite asset class—stocks, bonds, real estate, comic books, etc. Do-it-yourselfers are notorious for putting all their eggs in one basket: a 2003 survey of fourteen million US households determined that the average number of stocks in investors' portfolios was between one and five. Robo-advisors not only ensure your portfolio includes a carefully monitored mix of asset classes, but also ensure broad diversification.

While virtually every robo-advisor boasts about its Nobel Prize-winning investment strategy, they're all hanging their hats on the same research: Harry Markowitz's modern portfolio theory, or MPT. Markowitz published a paper in 1952 in the *Journal of Finance*, "Portfolio Selection," which presented a mathematical way to construct investment portfolios offering the maximum return for any given level of risk. The main lesson of MPT is that by diversifying your portfolio, you can reduce the overall risk for any given level of return, a compelling objective for most investors.

One of the best explanations of MPT that I've read is Burton Malkiel's in *A Random Walk Down Wall Street*. He describes an island economy with only two investments: an umbrella manufacturer, whose owner prays for rain, and a beach resort where business booms in sunny weather. The expected return for each business is the same, but an investor who choses one over the other is making a huge bet on the weather. By investing in both, he achieves the same return but reduces his risk to zero. To make this work in real life, however, you need to know how different investments move in relation to one another, called *correlation*, which is difficult to quantify and changes over time. Panics seem to sink all ships at the same time—"all correlations go to one"—although whether that's true or not is debatable. In any case, even in Malkiel's simple example, investments may not perform as expected, and the island investor may not achieve his expected return: "When there is a recession and people are unemployed, they may buy neither summer vacations nor umbrellas."[23]

Markowitz's model doesn't tell you *how* to build a diversified portfolio; it's simply a mathematical proof of the benefit of diversification. So while robo-advisors' marketing messages are superficially similar, pledging alliance to MPT, low costs, and hassle-free investing, their underlying investment methodologies can vary dramatically. The number of different ETFs per portfolio may be six, sixteen, or even more; and more asset classes is not necessarily better, as they can cancel each other out. Some portfolios stick with plain vanilla stock and bond ETFs, while others include assets such as real estate investment trusts (REITs) and precious metals funds, arguing that these improve diversification. Critics say these only add to the cost, as management expense ratios are typically higher for more specialized ETFs.

Other portfolio construction decisions that vary between robo-advisor include which specific ETFs are included, how often the portfolios are rebalanced, and how the firm defines terms like "conservative," "moderate," or "aggressive." Even the definition of an asset class varies; US equities may be split into subclasses such as small and large cap, growth and value, and so forth. Most robo-advisors disclose their investment methodologies in detail on their websites, however, so consumers willing to invest the time can look under the hood.

Early on, some worried that robo-advisors' catchy names and friendly websites might mislead consumers into believing their investment advice was somehow safer, that consumers might fail to realize that robo-portfolios, just like other investments in stocks and bonds, can decline in value. Probably the most practical advice Betterment received from the judges at TechCrunch Disrupt 2010 was from Marissa Mayer—at the time a rising star at Google, later CEO of Yahoo!—who warned Jon Stein to make sure his customers understand the risk.

In fact, Stein's description of Betterment as a replacement for your savings account dominated the discussion on TechCrunch's comments page. "This is completely irresponsible," wrote one self-described manager of more than $4 billion. "YOU CANNOT 'SELL' THIS AS A SAVINGS ACCT REPLACEMENT!!! You're going to get sued." Another loved the goal but not the path: "Any startup that involves money makes netizen hesitant to put their trust on it, for it turn out to be that next promising scam again." Robert Mah, one of the few critics willing to sign his name, predicted lawsuits and fraud charges, perhaps even handcuffs for Stein and his friends, while "Joe W." called Betterment criminal: "not only are they going to get sued into oblivion, the SEC will probably be shutting them down after customer complaints. Wow, is this dangerous! I can't believe anyone thought this was a good idea."[24]

While the discussion stopped short of proving Godwin's law ("As an online discussion grows longer, the probability of a comparison involving Nazis approaches"), Stein and his buddies were soundly flamed, pronounced dead on arrival, and charged with various crimes ranging from fraud to highway robbery. Surprised by the vehemence of the reaction, the team talked it over and decided Mayer and the trolls had a point: Betterment is not a replacement for your savings account. It's simply a better way to invest.

Since Betterment launched in 2010, choices for investors seeking automated portfolio management have multiplied like beer cans on a frat house lawn. Assets in US robo-advisors grew from zero to almost $100 billion by 2016.[25] This rapid growth has been fueled by hundreds of millions of dollars in venture capital. If the pattern of other technological innovations persists, expect a mass cull a few years from now. In *The Nature of Technology: What It Is and How It Evolves*, economist W. Brian Arthur describes the boom and subsequent bust of railways in mid-1840s Britain. Inevitably the initial frenzy subsides, with a few strong competitors emerging and building out their businesses in a new period of "sobriety and hard work, of confidence and steady growth."[26]

Early US railways got a boost from new technology—the Bessemer process—that dramatically reduced the price of steel. Henry Phipps Jr. and Andrew Carnegie licensed the technology for their startup, Carnegie Steel. "Iron production in the United States soared from 38,000 to 180,000 tons in the decade between 1850 and 1860," writes Arthur, leading to dramatic changes in the prices of wheat, hogs, and other supplies that could now be moved around the country more cheaply.[27] After Phipps and Carnegie sold their company twenty-nine years later, Phipps started an investment firm with the proceeds, to invest in entrepreneurial ventures like his own, named in honor of Lord Henry Bessemer, the inventor who patented the Bessemer process.[28]

Over the past hundred years, Bessemer Venture Partners has grown dramatically, with $4.5 billion now invested around the world. They've supported successful startups including Staples, Sports Authority, LinkedIn, and Skype. A few months after TechCrunch Disrupt 2010, Bessemer became the first outside investor in Betterment.

In February 2015, Jon Stein sent an email to his customers, thanking them for their support and announcing that the company had raised an additional $60 million to continue its growth. He predicted a day in the future when automated investing would be "as ubiquitous as automobiles," when the name "robo-advisor" would "sound as antiquated as calling cars 'horseless carriages.'"[29]

I'm not convinced Stein will ever shake that "robo" label. "Automated investing service" just doesn't have the same zip. And I'm not sure "robo-advisor" is even an insult at this point. When I think of robo-advisors, I think of transparency, user-friendliness, efficiency, and relentless cheerfulness no human being could ever hope to sustain. Robo-advisors have also gained credibility since big guns such as Morgan Stanley, Wells Fargo, Charles Schwab, and Vanguard launched automated portfolio offerings of their own, forced to follow the new generation's footsteps in the interest of self-preservation.

By the end of 2017, Betterment was managing $12 billion. Now in New York's Flatiron District, a.k.a. Silicon Alley, the company's 220 or so employees occupy three floors, the largest tenant in their building. Early criticisms have been addressed. No longer "a replacement for your savings account," Betterment is now "Investing Made Better." Ross, the chef, cooks breakfast on Mondays; lunch Wednesdays and Fridays. Show and Tell starts at 5 p.m. Friday afternoon, followed by Happy Hour. A dog-friendly workplace with an arsenal of snack food and Joyride Cold Brew coffee on tap, a nap room, and walls you can write on, no one would mistake this for a traditional investment firm.

As an undergrad at Harvard, Stein ran the Dunster Grille, the perfect place for a post-party snack, featuring nothing healthy, almost everything fried. The menu at Betterment is definitely better quality and better for you. But he considers his experience at the Grille good training for running Betterment, where he's often hiring and managing friends. As house bartender at his 350-person Harvard dorm, Stein organized social events, bringing students together and building confidence in his ability to get things done. Not every idea was a winner, of course. Like the time he organized a 3 a.m. trip to New Hampshire to go sledding with a few friends. "The trails were closed, so Jon towed people around on an icy road as they sat on dining hall trays holding onto jumper cables that hung from the back of his Jeep," one of his roommates later told the *Harvard University Gazette*.[30] "I have a long-time belief that if you have a crazy idea and you just have some conviction, you can probably get it done," laughs Stein. "Knocking on wood, I haven't got into too much trouble yet."

Back at TechCrunch Disrupt 2010, that shiny silver trophy went home with Soluto, an Israeli startup that's since been sold to a large Nashville-based firm. Betterment won Best in New York, not first prize but enough to put them on the radar screens of venture capitalists, enough to raise the money they needed to keep building out their platform. And with no mess, no bewilderment, and almost no sleep the night before, they signed up more than 300 customers their very first day.[31]

7

Wolves in Chic Clothing

"IS SHERYL HERE?" asks the president, searching the auditorium for her face. "There she is! Sheryl, stand up just so we know where you are." The crowd applauds as Sheryl Garrett stands, stunned to find herself in the spotlight.

It's February 2015 and Barack Obama is speaking to the Save Our Retirement Coalition at AARP headquarters, just around the corner from the White House. The AARP, formerly known as the American Association of Retired Persons, has thirty-seven million members, more than one in ten Americans.

"We're proud of Sheryl," says President Obama. "So I'm quoting you, Sheryl. Sheryl says, 'The role of a financial advisor is one of the most important jobs. But there is a segment of the industry today that operates like the gunslingers of the Wild West. We don't have the rules and regulations to protect those who we're supposed to be serving.' Couldn't have said it better myself."[1]

Garrett is known for saltier sound bites than this. She's compared financial planning to a colonoscopy, when often a routine checkup will do. The poster woman for fee-only financial advice, Garrett is founder of the Garrett Planning Network, 250 or so advisors who offer advice with no commissions, no conflicts of interest, and no minimum account size.

As a teenager in Kansas, Garrett devoured every issue of *Money* magazine. A chance meeting with a female financial advisor inspired her to leave her job as a college admissions counselor and sign up for a three-month boot camp at a financial services company. As soon as she was trained and registered to sell securities, Garrett's boss handed her a phone book and told her to get busy. "We were supposed to make 100 cold calls a day. I was there two years and I might have made 100 cold calls the whole time." Calling folks at dinner time to flog financial products just didn't sit right; Garrett felt queasy every Monday. She failed so miserably she was audited by the IRS, which questioned how she could survive on her reported $880 taxable income ("My roommate, Daddy, and credit cards").[2]

As a commissioned salesperson, Garrett wasn't subject to a fiduciary standard, a legal requirement to act in her clients' best interests. "I didn't even know the word fiduciary at the time," she says. She worked for a well-known firm, not a boiler room, and was never asked to do anything illegal. But when a couple asked for advice on where to hold their spare cash, she knew the best solution was a low-cost money market fund or savings account. The closest thing Garrett's employer offered was a ten-year certificate of deposit with a penalty if they cashed out early. Forced to choose between doing the right thing and getting paid, she knew it was time to leave. Garrett joined a financial planning firm, where she worked toward her Certified Financial Planner (CFP) designation.

Like the Chartered Financial Analyst (CFA) designation for investment professionals, the CFP requires years of work, challenging exams, and commitment to a professional code of conduct. Both CFPs and CFAs pledge to act in their clients' best interests. While the CFA and CFP are gold-standard professional credentials, they're easily confused with like-sounding but less-stringent certifications such as the CRFA, or Certified Retirement Financial Advisor, for example, which can be earned at a four-day seminar. Even when you do see "CFA" or "CFP" on someone's business card, the US Securities and Exchange Commission (SEC) recommends you verify those credentials independently, as well as checking the advisor's licensing and registration online.[3]

Credentials aren't the only pitfall on the path to sound advice. Consumers are often misled by wolves in chic clothing. A 2014 public awareness campaign showed a well-dressed clean-shaven man pitching investment advice to a roomful of prospective clients. "Would you trust me as your financial advisor?" he asks. When his prospects reply yes, he clicks a remote control, cuing a video clip of himself in his *real* job. Wearing a leather vest with no shirt, he's actually a professional DJ. "I have no financial experience at all," he says, dancing around the conference table. The ad ends with a voiceover: "If they're not a CFP pro, you just don't know."

According to the US Financial Planning Coalition, in addition to more than 70,000 qualified CFP professionals in the US, another 100,000 or so "incorrectly self-identify" as planners. Across North America, except in the Canadian province of Quebec—where you must meet specific educational requirements—anyone can call themself a "financial advisor" or "financial planner." Max Tailwag'er, a young Colorado-based dachshund, earned a listing in *The 2009 Guide to America's Top Financial Planners*. Max's owner, Allan Roth, is a Registered

Investment Adviser (RIA), a Certified Financial Planner (CFP), and Certified Public Accountant (CPA). He received a letter from an organization called the Consumers' Research Council of America informing him that he'd qualified for a listing in the guide. The letter wasn't addressed to Roth or even to his correct address, so he signed up his puppy to demonstrate how easily anyone with a valid credit card can bolster a resume with bogus achievements.

As an RIA, Roth is a fiduciary, required to act prudently, in good faith, and in his clients' best interests. Conflicts must be avoided and all material facts disclosed. A Registered Investment Advisor is a business or individual registered either with the Securities and Exchange Commission (SEC) or state securities regulators. RIAs are governed by the Investment Advisers Act of 1940, legislation born out of the stock market crash of 1929. (The wheels of government moved slowly even back then.) The second main category of US financial advisor is the broker-dealer—traditional stockbrokers. Since "broker" has become a dirty word, most have re-branded themselves with more genteel titles: wealth manager, account executive, financial advisor.

Unlike SEC-regulated Registered Investment Advisors, US broker-dealers are governed by the Financial Industry Regulatory Authority (FINRA), a self-regulatory organization. Also unlike RIAs, broker-dealers are not fiduciaries. Instead, they're held to a standard of suitability, the same standard that applies to most Canadian advisors. What's suitable for you may be less than ideal. Consider the range of suitable spouses: every man or woman who meets your basic criteria in terms of age, gender, physique, religion—whatever's on your wish list. Maybe anyone suitable will do, but most of us are more selective.

Overall, the North American financial services industry operates under a complicated patchwork of rules and regulations, making consumer education and protection even more challenging than if each country had a single regulatory regime.

Most Canadian advisors are registered with one of two self-regulatory organizations, the Mutual Fund Dealers Association (MFDA) or the Investment Industry Regulatory Organization of Canada (IIROC). Some are members of Advocis, a financial planning organization with roots in the insurance industry. Different advisors are licensed to sell different products, so their licensing may limit what investment options you're offered.

While earning her CFP and establishing herself as a full-fledged financial planner, Sheryl Garrett worked at a firm focused exclusively on high-net-worth clients. The intention wasn't to be elitist: the average consumer doesn't need the same level of service, and most can't afford it anyway. Still, Garrett was uncomfortable turning away middle-class folks like herself, her friends, and her family, and everyone else who didn't meet the firm's minimum account size.

So in 1998, she set out on her own to serve clients more concerned about car payments than custom-made suits or Cartier watches. People told Garrett she wouldn't survive selling advice by the hour, but she discovered almost immediately that normal-net-worth Americans were desperate for help. One woman left a tearful message on Garrett's machine after being turned down by every planner on her list because she had "only" $435,000.

"It just pulled my heart out," Garrett recalls, "to think that someone is apologizing for accumulating only $435,000. I called her back the next morning and I said 'Honey, I don't care if you have $4.35. I will talk to you and try to help you.'" Much of Garrett's early business came from other advisors referring clients who didn't meet their minimums or weren't interested in paying an ongoing percentage of assets, the conventional industry fee structure.

Four years into her new venture, Garrett had added three CFPs and 600 or so clients. When a trade publication featured her on its cover, her phone started ringing. Other advisors wanted help switching their own businesses to a no-minimum fee-based fiduciary model. She founded the Garrett Planning Network to share her strategies for success with others similarly inspired to serve the 85% or of Americans unable to meet minimum account sizes of $100,000 or more.[4]

By 2018, the network had grown to nearly 250 advisors, "self-employed, but never alone." Independence can be like going braless, says Garrett: all freedom and no support. Rather than a strictly standardized franchise model, her organization is a community of peers, less restrictive than a full-figure no-bounce underwire but more professional than a tube top. Some members are relatively new to the business while others are experienced pros who, like Garrett, have taken significant pay cuts to switch to a business model better aligned with their lifestyles and values. Today, Garrett no longer advises clients herself. In addition to running the network, she offers expert testimony in lawsuits, and operates a vacation resort: four log cabins in Eureka Springs, Arkansas, population 2,000—the honeymoon capital of the Ozarks.

One Friday in February 2015, she got a call from Washington, DC, inviting her to a press conference the following Monday, hosted by The Save Our Retirement Coalition, a group including the AARP (probably the largest fiduciary fan club in the world), as well as the 12.5-million-member American Federation of Labor and Congress of Industrial Organizations (AFL–CIO), and the Consumer Federation of America. She flew out Sunday night, unsure of what to expect. The crowd included a few familiar faces, people she knew from her work with the Committee for the Fiduciary Standard, an industry group formed in 2009. About ten minutes into his remarks, Obama suddenly called on Garrett. "Everything shifted," she remembers. "It was just brain-spinning." At home in Eureka Springs the next day, she watched the video to catch the end of his speech. She never imagined that the road from Kansas might lead to the White House.

Despite the president's support, the fiduciary rule didn't go through, drowned in a morass of conflicting expert opinions. While Garrett and her allies believe the rule would better protect investors, opponents argue that a uniform fiduciary standard would discourage advisors from serving small investors, raising costs and fueling frivolous lawsuits, thus reducing consumer access to advice. In fact, one study of four US states that have already adopted a fiduciary standard found "no statistical differences between the two groups [fiduciary states and non-fiduciary ones] in the percentage of lower-income and high-wealth clients, the ability to provide a broad range of products including those that provide commission compensation, the ability to provide tailored advice, and the cost of compliance."[5]

As Garrett's own experience suggests, many mainstream consumers are already priced out of the market due to high minimums at financial advice firms. In 2012, for example, Merrill Lynch stopped paying advisors to provide advice to new clients with accounts smaller than $250,000.[6] Ironically, Merrill itself was once a pioneer in reaching out to ordinary Americans. In 1946, the firm hired Louis Engel, a former *Business Week* reporter, as advertising director. Engel's first effort was a six-thousand-word *New York Times* advertorial "What Everybody Ought to Know about This Stock and Bond Business." Almost seven thousand readers responded. The ad ran for ten years, generating more than three million leads and making at least one author's list of the one hundred best ads of all time, alongside RCA's "His Master's Voice" and Coca-Cola's "The Pause that Refreshes."[7] However, even back in the '50s, mainstream consumers weren't attractive clients for most brokers; Merrill Lynch was taking on clients competitors didn't want, betting that some of these small fish would grow into whales.[8]

Because most advisors charge a percentage of client assets, large accounts are proportionately more profitable. But as your money grows, your fees usually do too, regardless of whether your need for advice increases at the same pace. Advisors who charge hourly fees can't count on the regular revenue stream of a percentage arrangement, since their clients decide how much advice they want. Hourly fees may also seem high to consumers used to paying "only" 1% or 2%, unaware of their true annual cost in dollar terms. In fact, many investors believe they pay nothing at all, especially in Canada where the cost of advice is typically embedded in fund expense ratios. Even when 2017 regulatory reforms required investment firms to report these costs to clients in dollar terms, more than 60% of clients continued to believe that the advice was free.[9]

Good advice can pay for itself many times over, through wiser decisions about taxes, insurance, retirement, college savings—even chasing your dreams. Years ago in a Minnesota library, a woman asked Sheryl Garrett for investment advice. She had two daughters in college, a low-paying job, and $50,000 or so in savings. When Garrett discovered that her lifelong dream was to go to nursing school, she advised the woman to follow her heart, spending her money on tuition and living expenses while she earned her degree. With nurses in short supply and commanding attractive starting salaries, the woman's best investment was in herself.

While robo-advisors offer a cheap and simple solution for investing, they won't hear your heart calling, and risk questionnaires don't measure the risk of failing to live life to the fullest. Behavioral finance expert Meir Statman says the best advisors are like skilled physicians, who listen empathetically for the clues they need to make an accurate diagnosis and deliver more than just medical care. "Patients leave the offices of good physicians not only with prescriptions that promote their health but also with the sense of well-being that comes from understanding the diagnosis, dire as it might be, and knowing the way forward."[10]

Just as avoiding the doctor can lead to health problems, ignoring financial planning can have serious consequences. In 2000, professional football star Derrick Thomas died suddenly at age thirty-three without a will, sparking a legal battle among the five mothers of his seven children. His agent had urged Thomas to see a planner. "We tried to set him up to do it ten times. The sad truth is that there was a certain group of athletes who actually believed that if they ever sat down to write their wills, they were going to die."[11]

While Thomas had more money—and more families—than most of us, failing to follow sound advice is common. In a 2009 study, 8,000 German brokerage clients were offered free unbiased financial advice. Only about 5% accepted the offer, and those who did were older, wealthier, and more financially sophisticated than the folks who turned it down. Yet only about a third of clients who received recommendations actually followed them, and even then, only partially. The advice turned out to be valuable too; over the ten months following the study, the recommended portfolios not only outperformed clients' actual holdings by more than 6%, they were also less volatile and better diversified. The authors concluded that consumer education is not an effective tool for helping investors make better decisions, citing an English proverb dating back to 1175: "You can lead a horse to water but you can't make it drink."

As more advisors recognize the benefits of fiduciary advice, swarms of so-called breakaway brokers are fleeing Wall Street firms to join the ranks of the independents. Brian Hamburger, a New Jersey lawyer, has built a successful business helping breakaway brokers. In 2007, he launched MarketCounsel Summit, a conference for Registered Investment Advisors. Thirty-five advisors met in a New Jersey hotel, sharing the venue with a Tenafly, New Jersey, girls' volleyball team. "Lunch was a donut," one former presenter joked.

Seven years later, we're scarfing down smoked salmon from bento boxes at the Four Seasons Las Vegas. The agenda is bursting with industry influencers and business celebrities including tech billionaire and Dallas Mavericks owner Mark Cuban; Eliot Spitzer, once known as "The Sherriff of Wall Street"; CNBC's Ron Insana; plus a pair of former SEC chairmen, Christopher Cox and Harvey Pitt.

Celebrity-whisperer Tony Robbins is the keynote speaker opening night, revving up a roomful of jet-lagged businessfolk with his passion for human potential. By the three-hour mark, well past bedtime back on the East Coast, five hundred or so financial advisors are jumping up and down shouting with joy. Robbins wraps up with a few words about his new book, *Money: Master the Game, 7 Simple Steps to Financial Freedom*, which emphasizes the value of fiduciary advice while at the same time financing a hundred million meals for hungry Americans (Robbins is donating all profits from the book to charity).

Similarly, Mark Cuban is here because he cares. He has declined a speaker's fee and even a lift from the airport. For Hamburger, the invitation to Cuban was a long shot. "I wrote a very personal email about the tremendous [RIA] business and how we work with the good guys—the guys who are fighting Wall Street," Hamburger told RIABiz.com. Guessing at Cuban's email address, he hit send and within the hour, Cuban replied "I'm in. Thanks for including me."[12]

Hamburger likes watching the sparks fly. That's why he put Cuban on stage with Christopher Cox, Chairman of the SEC when Cuban was accused of insider trading. Cuban spent eight years and $20 million defending his name. Offered a settlement, he kept fighting, just on principle, believing he was being unfairly targeted as a high-profile trophy for government lawyers. When a jury finally declared him not guilty, Cuban tells us, he went out and got "stinking drunk."

Cox, a defender of government bureaucracy, is lawyerly, polite, and a touch apologetic. Cuban, in jeans, sneakers, and NBA socks, grills Cox on the failings of his former employer. While suffering through his ordeal, worrying what he'd tell his kids if he lost, Cuban studied SEC transcripts from other cases to see if his own experience was normal. He tells Cox he thinks the SEC is worthless and that the only way to fix it is to burn it down and start from scratch. As he speaks, the audience erupts in a frenzy of tweeting, crashing the Four Seasons Wi-Fi network. Strangely, after an hour on stage together, Cox and Cuban seem like old friends.

While the industry argues about the costs and benefits of a uniform standard, two-thirds of consumers mistakenly believe stockbrokers are already fiduciaries, and three-quarters say the same about all financial advisors.[13] Reading the fine print just doesn't come naturally for most of us, and we're often tempted to trust our gut instincts, unaware that, regardless of our intelligence, we're surprisingly easy to manipulate.

For example, clothing confers authority; many more pedestrians will follow a jaywalker dressed in a suit than the same man in casual clothes. "Like the children of Hamelin who crowded after the Pied Piper, three and a half times as many people swept into traffic behind the suited jaywalker," writes psychologist and marketing professor Robert Cialdini. "In this case, though, the magic came not from his pipe but his pinstripes."[14]

When we're swayed by a person's charisma, physical attractiveness, or expensive clothing, we're likely to make bad decisions, forming a favorable impression based on factors that have nothing to do with the person's professional competence.

And when an advisor treats us to dinner or free tickets to a sporting event, we feel obliged to accept their advice, forgetting who really pays for these perks.

"When I was a big-shot," writes Henry Blodget. "I got passes to an air-conditioned suite in Arthur Ashe Stadium with a television and cheese plates. The next year, as I was falling from grace—like a stone—I got a seat so far up that I had to watch the match on the stadium screen." As a Wall Street celebrity during the dot-com bubble, Blodget wrote reports on the giddiest stocks of the day. His fortune faded fast when an investigation revealed he'd been encouraging clients to buy the same stocks he soundly disparaged in internal emails, calling them "junk," "shit," and "crap." Tossed out of the industry, he moved his own money to low-cost index funds. "Since switching to Vanguard, of course, I have watched the Open from my kitchen table."[15]

Eliot Spitzer, New York State Attorney General at the time, was Blodget's nemesis. Prior to his adventures on Wall Street, Spitzer waged successful battles against industrial polluters and pharmaceutical companies selling dangerous drugs. He ran a Garment District sweatshop for a year or so, a sting operation targeting the Gambino family.[16] At one time, Spitzer was viewed by some as potentially America's first Jewish president, but his political career came to an embarrassing halt when his own secrets were revealed. Spending thousands of dollars on high-priced hookers didn't square with his public image of Mr. Clean, and he resigned from his job as Governor of New York in 2008.

The hero-to-zero stories of Blodget the two-faced stock promoter and Spitzer the morally compromised crusader are vivid illustrations of the yin-yang quality of human nature. While morality is in the eye of the beholder—"we boil at different degrees" in Emerson's words—human beings are often hopelessly hooked by our emotions, regardless of our intelligence, education, and even our own better judgement. Protecting us against our own bad choices is a challenge for regulators.

One of the main tools for investor protection is mandatory regulatory disclosure. According to experts, simple, easily digestible disclosure at the point of purchase is the most effective form; for example, a green, yellow, or red card posted on the front door of a restaurant, or the energy ratings of kitchen appliances. Unfortunately, this style of disclosure doesn't work well for financial products. As Martin Wheatley, former director of the UK's Financial Conduct Authority (FCA) has commented, "It's now commonplace for bank accounts, insurance contracts, mortgages and the like to have terms and conditions longer than *Hamlet*."[17] Regulators have responded with solutions such as simplified prospectuses and Canadian "Fund Facts," easy-to-read two-pagers on mutual funds, to help investors better understand their investments.

But sometimes shortcuts, like pinstripes, lead us in the wrong direction. Morningstar "stars," for example, are almost ubiquitous in mutual fund advertisements, despite the fact that Morningstar itself describes these as providing a backward-looking scorecard rather than a forward-looking tool for choosing funds. One independent study described the top "five-star" rating as "the kiss of death."[18] The researchers found that US equity funds awarded the full five stars saw a subsequent "severe" drop in performance over the next three years.

Yet investors mistakenly view five stars as a sign of future promise. One 2002 study found that when funds achieved a five-star ranking, they attracted inflows more than 50% above normal, while funds that lost stars saw significant outflows.[19] To provide better guidance for investors, the company now offers Morningstar Analyst Ratings: gold, silver, or bronze "medals" or a neutral or negative rating. These offer a qualitative opinion on the outlook for each fund's risk-adjusted performance relative to its peers or a relevant index. In its first five years, the system seemed to work, with gold-medal funds typically outperforming their peers and negatively-rated funds tending to lag.[20] Despite the success of the new system, however, the stars remain the most popular performance metric for mutual funds.

In addition to the problems of complexity and misinterpretation, regulatory disclosure may also offload responsibility to the investor ("Didn't you read the fine print?"). And researchers have discovered that disclosure can even encourage consumers to act against their own best interests. In one series of studies, subjects were offered the choice between Fund A and Fund B. Fund A was clearly more attractive, but when the advisor disclosed that he was paid more for selling Fund B, clients accepted his biased advice. Although their trust was now actually *reduced*, they felt obliged to help him out, behavior known as *reluctant altruism*. Natural human reciprocity compels us to want to return the favor when someone buys us a meal or otherwise creates a sense of social obligation. Furthermore, the research found that advisors gave *worse* advice after disclosing conflicts, now freed from feeling guilty about putting their own interests first, an effect called *moral license*.[21]

Even if we're black belts in consumer self-defense, however, few of us have the financial background to analyze investment products the same way we can compare cell phone plans or vacation packages. Financial advice is what economists call a *credence good*, like medical treatments, car repairs, and nutritional supplements. Inexpert consumers can never know for sure that they've made the right choice without the training or experience necessary to evaluate the quality and value of the services received.[22]

Getting the straight facts can be a challenge even for an investment professional. One advisor with whom I spoke on behalf of a friend amazed me with his ability to effortlessly dodge important questions about costs and performance. Another emphasized the priceless value of our relationship, forged over five minutes on the phone together. After boasting of his eighteen years' experience, he then either didn't know or refused to tell me the full cost of the mutual funds he was recommending. He quoted their expense ratios, but when I asked him repeatedly about the additional cost for advice, he insisted it was very small and nothing to worry about. "Humor me," I said. "You're sitting in front of your computer. Look it up." As it turned out, the advisor's fee was more than the cost of the funds. In other words, the total cost was more than double what he'd disclosed.

George Akerlof won the 2001 Nobel Prize in Economic Sciences for his work on the problems of asymmetric information, memorably illustrated through his description of the market for used cars. Because sellers have better information, buyers are easily cheated. Since Akerlof's paper "The Market for 'Lemons'" was published, so-called lemon laws have been passed in most jurisdictions to protect consumers. Just as a non-mechanic can't accurately evaluate a used car, most investors lack the patience and financial know-how to make sense of the reams of financial disclosure intended to protect them. Disclosure alone merely creates the illusion of a level playing field.

When I needed affordable independent financial advice, I went looking for the Canadian equivalent of Sheryl Garrett. My brokerage statements showed that I was paying US withholding tax on some of my investments, and I wasn't sure how the rules worked. The first advisor I spoke to offered fee-only advice, but rather than hourly advice, his initial engagement was a $2,700 financial plan. All I needed was a checkup, not a colonoscopy. I searched some more, but no one seemed to be selling what I wanted to buy.

After losing hope, I stumbled across a blurb for a seminar, "Failproof Finances Workshop with Shannon Simmons." From her website, Simmons sounded like Garrett's Canadian cousin, a CFP as well as a refugee from high-net-worth financial planning. She offered unbiased affordable advice on a flat fee-for-service basis. I clicked a link to book an Investment Portfolio Analysis, $350 plus tax.

Simmons works a few streetcar stops from my former office, farther from the financial district, however, and closer to West Queen West, once voted the world's second coolest neighborhood by *Vogue* magazine. The reception area, serving a beehive of flexible workspace options, reminds me of Betterment. I'm surrounded by millennials with MacBooks, working alone or meeting in clusters at rugged wooden tables, all dressed casually except for one oddball in a dress shirt and tie.

We meet in a tiny glass office at the top of four flights of stairs. Simmons has consolidated my mess of accounts onto one spreadsheet and highlighted everything in green, yellow, or red. She answers all my questions and provides a handy cheat sheet on how to maximize the tax efficiency of my overall portfolio. Like an annual physical that finds nothing wrong, the appointment is worth every penny in peace of mind alone. My action plan is to sit tight. Sometimes the best thing to do is nothing, and Simmons has no incentive to tell me any different.

Around the world consumers are educating themselves about the true costs of investing. Just as the Internet has transformed the used car business, this could radically alter the rules of the game. When my car was stolen in 2014, I went shopping for a replacement, not exactly my beloved 1992 Acura, but a late-model something-similar with minimal mileage. I shopped online, found a Honda that fit the bill, and headed for the showroom—knowing exactly what I was willing to pay. The salesman informed me right up front that he was paid on volume, not price, so we haggled a bit for appearance's sake, then did the deal. No one's going to win a Nobel Prize writing about the used car market nowadays. The conflict is all gone; it's downright cooperative.

Despite the efforts of personal finance columnists, financial literacy organizations, government regulators, and everyone else trying to make the world a safer place for investors, most of us spend more time reading free catalogues we receive in the mail than our own financial statements.[23] Our discomfort with complexity and the unfamiliar is compounded by the remarkable human ability to remain willfully blind to things we don't wish to see. Before investing our money, we need to invest the time and energy in reading the fine print, asking the hard questions, and learning to stop following Armani suits out into traffic.

Back in Eureka Springs, Sheryl Garrett refuses to buy clothing that needs to be ironed or dry cleaned, even to visit the president. She zips around the Ozarks in her sixteen-year-old Subaru Outback and lives in a log home with a swimming pool ("it came with the resort") where her daughter is learning to swim. Sometimes the best investment is to follow your heart.

8

Enough Is Enough

FOR THIRTY YEARS, Phil Ashburn worked for the phone company, first Western Electric, later Pacific Bell. At 51, he was offered a buyout. He could retire early—with either a pension of $1,500 a month for life or a $355,000 lump sum—or he could stay put. Facing the pivotal financial decision of his life, Ashburn sought help from a financial advisor who'd run seminars at his workplace.

"She told me the decision was easy and a no-brainer, that I should take the lump sum and allow her to invest it... [S]he promised I would never go broke, always have money, and even have money left for my family when I was gone."[1]

It's March 2015, and Ashburn is testifying at the Forum on Ending the Retirement Savings Drain and Improving Economic Security. He's telling his story to Senators Elizabeth Warren and Elijah Cummings and a roomful of others advocating for tougher laws governing financial advisors.

Told he and his wife could afford an income of up to $3,000 a month, Ashburn hired the advisor, selected the lump sum, and signed the money over for her to invest. "There were handshakes and hugs, then she left. As we watched her walk down the sidewalk, my wife and I never felt so elated. Our future was secure... what a relief!"[2]

A few years later, 80% of his money was gone, Ashburn tells the senators. He felt like a frog in hot water. "I didn't know I was getting cooked until it was too late." Today he's surviving on Social Security, part-time work as a dog trainer, and his wife's earnings. His former advisor lives in a gated community in Florida. When Ashburn's case eventually went to arbitration, he lost.[3]

Either through choice or necessity, working after retirement age is increasingly common. In 2017, almost 19% of Americans age sixty-five and older were still in the labor force.[4] In part, this may reflect the fact that Social Security was never intended as a full pension. The program is considered supplemental to personal savings, pensions, and insurance coverage. The Social Security Administration says a worker with average earnings can expect his or her retirement benefit to replace about 40% of average lifetime earnings.[5] (The Canada Pension Plan's retirement pension currently replaces around 25% of earnings, but that number is expected to increase to 33% in 2019.[6]) When Social Security was launched in 1935, the odds were in the government's favor: benefits began at age sixty-five at a time when average life expectancy was sixty-one.[7] Today, the combined impact of longer lives, stagnant wages, and high health-care costs mean fewer North Americans are able to save enough during our working years to support ourselves in old age, making government pensions an increasingly important source of income.

Social Security is the topic of a two-hour session at Bogleheads XIV, an annual convention/fan fest that attracts more than 200 of Jack Bogle's 30,000 online fans, a.k.a. The Bogleheads. They're the Deadheads of low-cost investing, mostly

Americans but one all the way from Taiwan. Bogle is the founder of Vanguard, pioneer of the retail index fund, which by one calculation has saved investors more than $100 billion in fees.[8] In 1974, Paul Samuelson, the first American economist to win a Nobel Prize, wrote a three-page essay in the inaugural issue of the *Journal of Portfolio Management* calling for the creation of "an unmanaged, low-turnover, low-fee index fund."[9] Bogle used the paper as Exhibit A to convince his board of directors to launch a business that now manages $5 trillion. Samuelson, in turn, has compared index funds to "the invention of the wheel, the alphabet, Gutenberg printing, and wine and cheese," and claimed to have trained his fifteen grandchildren to include Vanguard in their bedtime prayers.[10]

Bogleheads XIV is a labor of love for the half-dozen or so volunteers who've organized it. Most of the action takes place at a local hotel. Keep the name to yourselves, we're warned at the opening night cocktail party. If you're posting online, you can say you're at the "Philly Conference," no more. Someone "caused a ruckus" years ago, I'm told by one of the tribe. No elaboration is offered. We're not here to throw stones. Throughout the two-day event, I'm reminded of my first visit to Walt Disney World, where despite the crowds and lineups, everyone seemed enchanted just to be there.

Tickets went on sale in February and sold out in a few weeks. A reporter for *Kiplinger's Personal Finance* is here covering the conference, but with no ticket, he waits outside. No one enters without a ticket, and only Mr. Bogle himself gets in for free. Fair play and frugality are core tenets of the Bogleheads' philosophy. Most aspire to lifestyles of LBYM—living below your means.

When Bogle arrives, we stand and cheer. At eighty-six, he's still full of fight. He speaks with the unwavering idealism of a college student and the dauntless determination of a superhero. He jokes that his heart is only forty-five, referring to a 1996 transplant following multiple heart attacks, the first at age thirty. In 1967, Bogle was told by a cardiologist that he'd never work again.[11] He didn't listen, working almost full-time even while hospitalized for four months awaiting surgery.[12]

Failing health is the reason most people retire, rather than a desire to forgo wages for a life of repose. More than 40% of workers retire earlier than planned, about half for health-related reasons, and most others due to job loss.[13] Affluent men like Bogle are statistically the most likely to be working in old age.[14] Fortunately, finance requires no heavy lifting. Bogle's health hasn't ended his working career, which began at age nine, delivering magazines to help support his family. But Bogleheads XIV is held close to home, as he limits his travel these days.

At the 2015 conference, Bogleheads Mel Turner and Mike Piper, a writer and Certified Public Accountant (CPA), run through the nuts and bolts of Social Security, then answer questions from the audience. Their main message is that almost everyone should wait as long as possible to claim retirement benefits. Full retirement age ranges from sixty-six to sixty-seven, depending on when you were born, but you can start receiving benefits as early as age sixty-two.[15] Claiming early reduces your monthly check by as much as 30%. Alternatively, you can wait until you're seventy and receive as much as 30% *more*. In one example, a retiree who'd be entitled to $1,000 a month at full retirement gets only $750 by claiming early. Holding out to age seventy, he would have received $1,320 a month.[16] The government calculates payments using actuarial tables designed to ensure fairness, aiming to pay out the same amount over your lifetime regardless of when payments start. (Note that the rules and amounts are subject to change; this information is from 2015.) About 40% of people claim as soon as they qualify, permanently reducing the size of their checks.[17] Piper tells us the actuarial assumptions baked into the government's calculations are out of date, so we're likely to come out ahead by waiting.

Regardless of when you claim, Social Security is one of the safest sources of retirement income, guaranteed by the government and indexed to inflation. Inflation risk is significant when you're planning two or three decades into the future; $1,000 decays to only $670 after twenty years of 2% inflation, $545 after thirty. At 4%, $1,000 is worth only about $295 after thirty years. People who claim early and live to age 100 or more may regret settling for smaller checks for all those years, while those who wait but then die before age seventy may also regret their decision. Some experts recommend claiming early only if you're in poor health or in urgent need of the money.

Do-it-yourselfers at heart, the Bogleheads debate the merits of various Social Security guides and online calculators. But this is a one-time decision with profound consequences, so spending a few hundred dollars on a professional opinion is recommended. The decision is complicated by dependents, divorces, and deceased spouses. Married couples need to consider the health of each spouse, their age differential, different income levels, and more. The options are mind-boggling, even for the staunchly self-reliant Bogleheads.

Canadians face the same decision when applying for benefits from the Canada or Quebec Pension Plans (CPP/QPP). In 2015, normal retirement age was sixty-five, but you could apply for benefits as early as age sixty, receiving almost 40% less, or wait until age seventy, gaining a 40% bonus. Additional programs are available to supplement lower incomes: Old Age Security (OAS) and Guaranteed Income Supplement (GIS). Once universal, OAS benefits are now taxed back from higher income earners, "clawed back" in the passive-aggressive vernacular of Canada. While US benefits are based on your thirty-five best earnings years, Canadian CPP considers your whole work history, allowing you to drop your eight worst years, or more in certain situations. As a result, some advisors recommend claiming early if you expect to finish your career with a large number of low- or zero-earnings years.

From the podium, Bogle recalls the lean years—the lean decade, actually—after Vanguard launched the first retail index fund in 1976. The fund set out to raise $150 million but attracted less than a tenth of that, earning the nickname "Bogle's Folly."[18] Early on, index funds were viewed as subversive. Critics called them un-American. "I can't believe that the great mass of investors are going to be satisfied with just receiving average returns," said Fidelity Chairman Edward "Ned" Johnson III. "The name of the game is to be the best."[19] Over time, however, "just average" has attracted increasing numbers of investors, transforming Vanguard from David into Goliath, and prompting Fidelity to launch index funds of its own.

Bogle boasts that his net worth—estimated around $80 million—is dwarfed by Johnson's, rumored in the $7 billion range. It's a point of pride for a man whose last car was an 1987 Acura.[20] His creation of Vanguard has been described as an act of unprecedented generosity. "It's almost as if Ford or Procter & Gamble issued shares to the people who bought their cars and soap, or if Bill Gates had given away a piece of Microsoft to each purchaser of Windows," investment expert Bill Bernstein told the *Journal of Indexes* in a 2012 issue dedicated exclusively to Bogle.[21] What's unique about Vanguard is that the company itself is owned by its customers. It's the only remaining mutual fund company that's still truly mutual, owned by the investors in its funds rather than by separate public shareholders.

Of Bogle's many books, *Enough: True Measures of Money, Business, and Life* is the most overtly philosophical, lamenting a world with too much speculation, complexity, and salesmanship; not enough investment, simplicity, and stewardship. When asked, "How much is enough?", Bogle offers Horace's definition: anywhere between the poverty of a hovel and the envy of a palace. For practical purposes, however, most of us need to narrow it down. Not only do we need to consider how much to stash away as savings during our working years, but when we eventually start spending those savings, we face the challenge of estimating how much we can safely spend without jeopardizing our long-term financial security.

This problem was considered solved in 1994 when financial planner Bill Bengen used Monte Carlo simulation to evaluate the probability of running out of money over a thirty-to-fifty-year time horizon. His solution—4%—became an industry rule of thumb that's still widely used by planners and financial planning software. But most use it incorrectly. Bengen intended the number as a starting point, with adjustments up or down to reflect an individual's expected longevity and risk tolerance. And the 4% rate applied only to year one; fine-tuning was required in subsequent years to reflect changes in the cost of living.

During the bull market of the late 1990s, Bengen was criticized for being overly conservative. After the crash of 2000, however, critics said 4% was too generous, assuming optimistic investment returns based on historical averages that had been skewed upward by the tech bubble. Also, the model assumed a constant 50/50 mix of stocks and bonds—more aggressive than most retirement portfolios. An academic paper published in 2013 calculated that at then-current interest rates, following the 4% rule was a recipe for ruin, exposing retirees to a 60% risk of running out of money over the next thirty years.[22]

In 2012, Bengen back-tested his model for every thirty-year period since 1926 to evaluate his strategy's long-term performance. He discovered that the worst outcome was for folks who retired in 1969. To maintain their lifestyles through the high inflation of the 1970s, they would have been forced to increase withdrawals to double-digit rates, decimating their savings. Bengen worried that future inflation might create a "worse-than-worst-case" scenario for retirees relying on his 4% rule. "Quite frankly," he wrote, "I am at a loss for a meaningful technique to forecast the upcoming years. My historical, deterministic approach doesn't seem particularly useful."[23] A year later, at age sixty-five, Bengen sold his business to spend more time with his wife, Cookie.

Despite the risk of running out of money in retirement, many of us can't seem to stop spending it, accumulating more stuff than we can ever possibly use. Psychologists explain this behavior through the theory of *getting begets wanting*.[24] Rather than satisfying our desire, getting what we want is like scratching a mosquito bite; the itch only gets worse. Hopping off the hedonic treadmill is the best remedy, say experts, rather than seeking satisfaction, which always remains slightly out of reach.

Buddhists figured this out centuries ago. Like drinking salt water to slake our thirst, our relentless pursuit of happiness only fuels more grasping, whether it's for love, money, or material possessions. Our new toys eventually lose their attraction. Or we suffer constant anxiety about losing what we've gained. As teacher Dzigar Kongtrül writes, "Because we can't hold both craving and contentment in our awareness at the same time, craving keeps us from appreciating who we are, where we are, and what we have."[25]

In the first or second century, Buddhist scholar Nagarjuna described generosity as the key to contentment, "the greatest wealth on earth."[26] Whether you agree with him or not, generosity can also pay off in terms of improved social status, tax deductions, and a psychological high. Donating money activates the same region of the brain that responds to art, beauty, and cocaine. And it's the ultimate low-cost investment—giving $5 can make you as happy as giving $20. Getting begets wanting, but giving begets happiness.

Yet most people mistakenly believe spending money on themselves makes them happier than spending money on others.[27] And spending money to signal status—with designer clothes, prestige cars, and monster homes—is no longer enough. Researchers Silvia Bellezza, Anat Keinan, and Neeru Paharia have described "a more nuanced kind of conspicuous consumption that operates by shifting the focus from the preciousness and scarcity of goods, to the preciousness and scarcity of individuals."[28] While that may sound like a step in the right direction, they're not talking about valuing friends and family. They're describing the glorification of the workaholic; busyness as a status symbol: "Busyness at work might speak to the intrinsic qualities and capabilities of the individual who, as a scarce and precious resource herself, is like a rare gemstone and thus perceived to have high status and is greatly admired." Apple CEO Tim Cook boasts of starting his day at 3:45 a.m. Elon Musk supposedly keeps a sleeping bag at the Tesla factory. Marissa Mayer once told an interviewer she worked 130-hour weeks in the early days of Google. Later, as CEO of Yahoo!, she worked from her hospital bed after her twins were born.

The same researchers found that in Europe, where vacation time is more highly valued, busyness was a sign of lower social status. Also, agency mattered; having no life is only a status symbol if it's self-imposed, not if you're working long hours to make ends meet. And in fact, while the wealthy whine about their busy lives, as a group, they're actually working fewer additional hours today than forty years ago compared to the lowest earners. According to the Economic Policy Institute, from 1979 to 2016, the number of hours worked by the wealthiest 20% of US workers increased by about 4%, while the lowest wage earners worked 24% more hours.[29]

The gaping divide between rich and poor actually drags us all down together. Studies show that in countries with a high level of income inequality, rates of illness and social problems are higher for *both* rich and poor. According to the authors of *The Spirit Level: Why Greater Equality Makes Societies Stronger*, inequality actually predicts social problems better than absolute wealth. Where the gap between the richest and poorest is wide, expect more mental illness, drug abuse, obesity, and incarceration. For instance, in Sweden, death rates and infant mortality rates were lower than they were in England and Wales, not just for low-income groups but for the wealthy as well.[30] Similar analysis was conducted using data comparing American states, with the same conclusion: inequality is unhealthy for everyone.

Back at Bogleheads XIV, someone asks Jack Bogle a question about Vanguard's future. "We need to make sure we don't forget the honest-to-God human beings," he replies, "each one with their own hopes and fears and goals." Bogle disdains the cry of the consultant—if you can measure it, you can manage it. "How do you measure character? How do you measure integrity? How do you measure loyalty?" Bogle himself has never mistaken life for a numbers game. For years, the odds seemed slim that he'd still be preaching to the converted at age eighty-six. Yet he's already outlived his twin brother David by more than twenty years.

Spending three days with the Bogleheads was a priceless adventure. Driving home through the postcard-perfect Pennsylvania countryside, I feel fortunate to be jobless, despite the fact I have no idea where I'm headed. The uncertainty feels genuinely liberating, unlike the false certainty of believing a

Maserati will make me happy. Clearly "enough" is not a number but a state of mind.

I take the long way home by accident, the scenic route instead of the interstate. But the sun's shining and the road is clear. And for now, that's enough.

9

The View from the Mountaintop

As MY SHUTTLE from the airport cruises up the driveway of the Broadmoor Resort, the giant pink hotel looms larger and larger, eventually eclipsing the spectacular Rocky Mountain scenery. This optical illusion triggers something in the back of my travel-scrambled brain, something about paving paradise. My room isn't ready, so I collapse in the coffee shop. With caffeine, my brain kicks back into gear, and I recall the lyrics to Joni Mitchell's classic, "Big Yellow Taxi."

I'm in Colorado Springs to attend the 2015 SRI Conference—"SRI" for Sustainable, Responsible, and Impact Investing. Today, the term is used interchangeably with the more sterile "ESG," which refers to considering environmental, social, and governance metrics alongside traditional financial ones. Being "green" doesn't come naturally to me. I raised two kids in disposable diapers, drink an endless river of bad-for-me soda from single-serve containers, and relentlessly fail to compost.

But I'm as awestruck by majestic mountains as anyone. After staring at a towering grove of eucalyptus trees for a single minute, students in one study scored higher on tests of helpfulness and ethicality than another group asked to stare at a tall office building. Scientists report that awe makes us feel small and less self-important, fostering collaborative behavior, generosity, and trust. Meeting on a mountaintop may boost the spirit of collaboration even before the conference begins.[1]

For years, SRI investing was a niche dismissed by Wall Street as the realm of tree-huggers and socialists, not serious financial folks. But suddenly the oddballs are the new in-crowd. I'm one of more than 600 attendees, and half of us are attending for the first time.

"I was country when country wasn't cool," jokes Frank Coleman, quoting a Barbara Mandrell song. Coleman is being honored as an industry pioneer at this year's conference. He's a senior executive at Christian Brothers Investment Services, an organization that manages $5 billion for Catholic institutions, aligning their portfolios with Catholic values by screening out companies that make products like birth control pills, pornography, and tobacco.[2] Additionally, Coleman's organization encourages companies to improve their performance on ESG-related issues by filing shareholder resolutions and engaging in dialogue with corporate leaders.[3]

Years ago, corporations weren't exactly rolling out the welcome mat for Coleman and his allies. He tells of attending the 1989 annual meeting of insurance company AIG. After presenting a shareholder proposal for increasing the diversity of the company's board of directors, "I turned around and realized I had a fifteen-foot radius around me. All the employees had moved away."

Filing shareholder resolutions may sound like pushing paper, but in fact, it's a powerful tool for changing the world, and a fundamental aspect of SRI investing. Back in the mid-1950s, Harvard law student Ralph Nader grew curious about automotive safety. His 1965 book *Unsafe at Any Speed* warned consumers about the "designed-in dangers" of American cars. Five years later, Nader succeeded in getting two issues on the ballot of the General Motors annual meeting, calling for stricter emissions standards and a better-diversified board of directors. While he lost both votes, he won the war; the media attention generated wider awareness of the lack of automobile safety and prompted GM to add an African American director, Reverend Leon Sullivan, to its board.

Life magazine had named Sullivan one of America's leading citizens in 1963 after he organized a boycott of Philadelphia businesses with racist hiring policies. Boycotts like Sullivan's played a central role in the American Civil Rights movement. Dr. Martin Luther King's Operation Breadbasket raised awareness of racism in hiring by targeting corporate giants like Sealtest, Coca-Cola, and Wonder Bread. By 1967, the program was credited with creating more than 2,000 new jobs in Chicago alone.[4]

Joining GM's board gave Sullivan an opportunity to take his activism global. At the 1971 GM annual meeting, the Right Reverend John Hines, Presiding Bishop of the Episcopal Church, asked the company to exit apartheid South Africa. GM was the largest employer of blacks in that country, as well as the largest employer in the US at the time.[5] Sullivan took up the cause, creating a code of conduct—the Global Sullivan Principles—that required US companies to desegregate their South African operations and offer equal pay and employment opportunities to non-whites, as well as better housing, health care, and education. While more than one hundred US multinationals signed on, many did not, leading to negative media attention, global boycotts, and eventually, the divestment campaign.

Some academic studies say divestment policies have no meaningful economic impact.[6] One found "little discernable effect" on South African banks, companies, or financial markets.[7] Yet the anti-apartheid movement was a spectacular success in raising public awareness, forcing corporations and governments to respond. By the late 1980s, the US, Canada, Japan, Israel, and the European Economic Community had all banned new investment in the country.[8]

South African divestment sowed the seeds of the current socially responsible investing movement. Over the years, new laws and regulatory requirements have demanded greater accountability and transparency from all corporations. Coleman and many others at the SRI Conference have played critical roles in making this happen, shining sunlight on once-secret data. Today, SRI is cool: companies are calling on the same folks they once steered clear of, eager for advice on how to meet investor demands for more information and better performance on environmental, social, and governance issues.

The category is growing faster than friendly bacteria. At the start of 2016, ESG factors influenced more than 20% of US industry assets—more than $8 trillion—up 33% from 2014.[9] This includes institutional investments such as pension funds, endowments, and foundations, as well as mutual funds, exchange-traded funds, and hedge funds. The number of SRI funds available to individual investors grew from 55 in 1995 to more than 1,000 in 2016, with assets increasing from $12 billion to more than $2.5 trillion.[10]

ESG products require the same careful due diligence as any investment, looking behind the label to the details of the investment strategy and underlying holdings. For instance, definitions of social responsibility vary widely; while Timothy Plan mutual funds exclude companies that "promote lifestyles contrary to biblical beliefs," the Workplace Equality Portfolio exchange-traded fund (EQLT) invests exclusively in companies that support lesbian, gay, bisexual, and transgender equity in the workplace. Funds from Dimensional Fund Advisors screen out companies that make contraceptives or engage in stem cell research, unusual outside explicitly faith-based funds. Some firms use both negative and positive screens, accentuating the positive and eliminating the negative, while others, such as the Dow Jones Sustainability Indices, take a "best in class" approach, including the top performers in each industry. As a result, investors may be surprised by some of the stocks they find in funds labeled socially responsible.

When BP's Deepwater Horizon oil rig blew up, burned, and sank, resulting in eleven deaths, a five-million-barrel spill, and widespread environmental destruction, BP shares were held in numerous SRI funds as well as the Dow Jones Sustainability Indices. The stock plunged more than 50% over the next few months. Defending an investment decision that proved embarrassing in hindsight, some fund managers argued that BP was a leader in a lousy industry. Yet the Deepwater disaster wasn't unprecedented. An explosion at a Texas refinery five years earlier had killed fifteen workers and injured dozens more, and one government official had described BP as a company with "systemic safety and health problems."[11]

Discovering the disconnect between our investment portfolios and our values was the topic of Clara Miller's presentation at the SRI Conference. In 2011, Miller became leader of the F.B. Heron Foundation, established in 1992 to help people help themselves out of poverty. When she examined the organization's investment portfolio, she was stunned to discover shares of Walmart, not a well-respected name among antipoverty activists. Owning the stock wasn't an act of hypocrisy, simply one of unawareness. Heron had invested in passively-managed index funds, inadvertently including holdings at odds with the foundation's mission.

Miller offers this as an illustration of one of the core problems of modern finance: separating our money from our mission. Heron's mission has become more challenging since the 2008 financial crisis. Poverty is now a tougher trap to climb out of. Americans need more than short-term help to buy homes or pay for education. They need jobs. So Miller committed Heron to investing "all in," fully aligning the foundation's assets with its mission.

Aligning money and mission is essential, not just to investors, but to society, according to the Governor of the Bank of England Mark Carney: "We need to recognize the tension between pure free-market capitalism, which reinforces the primacy of the individual at the expense of the system, and social capital, which requires from individuals a broader sense of responsibility for the system. A sense of self must be accompanied by a sense of the systemic."[12]

To Buddhists, selfishness and selflessness aren't opposites but two sides of the same coin; what benefits humanity benefits the individual. Clinging to self-interest is considered a recipe for unhappiness: "All the joy the world contains has come through wishing happiness for others. All the misery the world contains has come through wanting pleasures for oneself." Eighth-century Indian scholar Shantideva may sound like Pollyanna, but philosopher Robert Solomon argued the same thing in a 1993 essay: "For the properly constituted social self, the distinction between self-interest and social-mindedness is unintelligible, and what we call selfishness is guaranteed to be self-destructive as well. [T]he most serious single problem in business ethics is the false antagonism between profits and social responsibility."[13]

Emphasizing common interests may become more challenging for the SRI pioneers as large traditional financial firms move into their territory. Frank Coleman warns against the danger of discord. "The wonderful and unique diversity that we have among us is a gift and not an anchor," he says. As an African American and an investor guided by Catholic values, Coleman himself would add diversity to most investment conferences I've attended. Yet when he talks about values, I believe they're ones most of us in this audience share—saving the planet, preserving human dignity, forcing companies to consider the full impact of their operations. As Coleman concludes, the ballroom explodes in applause.

Faith-based investors like Coleman are the true pioneers of SRI. Well before mutual funds were invented, Jews, Christians, Muslims, and others avoided financial involvement in activities that violated their religious beliefs. In the mid-1700s, John Wesley, the founder of Methodism, advised his flock to make as much money as possible, but never at the expense of life or health. Avoid dangerous jobs, dishonest activities, and sinful trade, especially trafficking in "liquid fire" (alcohol), a poison that drives drinkers "to hell like sheep."[14]

In the 1960s, Methodist minister and educator Luther Tyson worked in Mississippi registering African Americans to vote. He fought for food stamps, welfare reform, and low-cost housing. During the Vietnam War, a woman in Ohio wrote him a letter asking where she might find a mutual fund that excluded war-related businesses. When Tyson came up empty-handed, he decided to start his own, working with fellow minister Jack Corbett. Tyson's wife Mary suggested the name "Pax," Latin for peace, although the new fund had a broader mandate, considering environmental and social factors as well. Thus, the Pax World Fund, later renamed the Pax World Balanced Fund, became the first socially responsible mutual fund.

Still, the question lingered as to whether socially responsible investing was responsible from the point of view of fiduciaries and investment advisors legally bound to act in their clients' best interests. Some experts maintain that any restriction on an investment universe reduces a portfolio's potential return, so by shunning "sin stocks," investors compromise their investment performance.

When Amy Domini, a Boston stockbroker, co-authored the first consumer guide to SRI investing in 1984, she wrote that the performance of these portfolios "flattens the limited choice argument." Her confidence was based more on personal conviction than hard numbers, though, with only a few flimsy data points to support her argument. Her interest in the area hadn't been driven by performance, however, but by client requests. "Occasionally clients would say to me, 'Ugh, I'd never buy a paper company. I'm an avid birder and the herbicides they use are killing songbirds.' Or, 'Ugh, what are you talking about coal? Have you ever seen a coal mine?'"[15] When she starting asking them, almost every client had non-financial values they wanted reflected in their portfolios. "'Dad died of lung cancer.' 'Brother died drunk on the highway.' 'Best friend died in 'Nam.'" Her book, *Ethical Investing: How to Make Profitable Investments without Sacrificing Your Principles*, made Domini the go-to expert in the field.

To answer the question of performance conclusively, Domini and two partners, Peter Kinder and Steven Lydenberg, devised a yardstick, the Domini 400 Social Index. They screened the US stock market for both positive and negative factors, building a model portfolio of companies scoring high on attributes like diversity, employee relations, and environmental stewardship, while excluding those causing more harm than good. At the end of February 2018, the index, now called the MSCI KLD 400 Social Index, had performed almost identically to the MSCI US IMI, the benchmark to which it's compared, 10.1% to 10.0%.

While Domini's index has proven her point that investors don't have to give up performance to invest responsibly, she and her partners didn't wait for the results to come in. In 1991, they created the Domini Impact Equity Fund, which over time evolved into Domini Impact Investments, an SEC-Registered Investment Advisor managing more than $2 billion at the end of 2017.

At the SRI Conference, Domini tells us that more than seventy-seven million children worldwide are no longer working in factories and farms after years of relentless advocacy by SRI shareholders, children who "would not have been liberated by enlightened consumers buying cool products." Their freedom came not from compassionate governments or better business practices, but from investors "taking a stand on an issue in a united way and pounding on it for twenty years." Also thanks to the SRI community, more than 7,500 companies around the world are publishing social responsibility reports, and ESG data is at the fingertips of most investment professionals through the industry's 325,000 Bloomberg terminals.

For years I was a value investor, seeking quality stocks at cheap prices. Only toward the end of my run as a fund manager did I make the connection with "values" investing, completing a certification in sustainable investing offered by a Montreal-based business school. All along, however, I'd believed that corporate governance is a valuable indicator of investment quality. A board of directors with no women, for instance, often reflects a clubby, close-minded corporate culture. I'd also always paid attention to social and environmental factors, although primarily for financial reasons: sweatshops and oil spills are simply bad business.

Over the past decade or so, academic studies have proven again and again that environmental, social, and governance information is valuable data for investors. The evidence is catalogued in meta-studies such as the 2015 paper "ESG and Financial Performance: Aggregated Evidence from More than

2,000 Empirical Studies," as well as reports such as Morgan Stanley's "Sustainable Reality: Understanding the Performance of Sustainable Investment Strategies," which looked at results for more than 10,000 US mutual funds and almost 3,000 separately managed accounts.[16]

In the past, bad corporate behavior has often gone unpunished. Traditional financial accounting ignores the true cost of *externalities*: pollution, social harm, and other costs of doing business borne by communities and the environment rather than the companies themselves. Today, ignoring ESG issues is dramatically riskier for both corporations and investors. Climate change, for example, is having significant effects on agriculture, tourism, and other industries. Scorching-hot summers in Bordeaux are threatening the region's $4 billion wine industry, causing grapes to ripen too early, making merlot taste like "a fruit bomb with no hard edges."[17] Companies are being forced to face the facts about their low-cost labor in faraway countries, after tragedies like the 2013 Rana Plaza factory collapse in Bangladesh that killed more than a thousand people. In 2015, a lawsuit was filed in California against Nestlé, as well as privately-owned Hershey and Mars, accusing the three of knowingly selling chocolate made with child labor in Ivory Coast.[18] Of course, the ultimate ESG risk is an equal-opportunity destroyer: the destruction of our environment in one big nuclear bang, or more slowly, by raising the temperature until every living thing is poached.

Due to the efforts of the SRI community and other activists, corporations are held to higher standards now than ever before. For example, the 1989 Exxon Valdez set a record for the worst man-made environmental disaster when it spilled eleven million barrels of oil into Prince William Sound. The original fine of $5 billion was eventually reduced to $900 million, plus $125 million in criminal fines. Twenty years later, BP faced much stiffer penalties following the Deepwater Horizon disaster. According to one estimate, the company spent more than $40 billion in clean-up costs in the first year alone, in addition to a $20.8 billion settlement with the US government, the largest in history.[19]

In 2005, a report commissioned by the United Nations concluded that integrating ESG factors into investment decisions was "clearly permissible and... arguably required."[20] Yet three years later, the US Department of Labor issued a bulletin interpreted by many fiduciaries as discouraging the use of non-financial investment information. At the SRI Conference, the crowd is celebrating a clarification published just days earlier, giving ESG investing a green light. Others in the industry are shaking their heads, however, viewing SRI as a campaign to pollute finance with politics and ideology, perhaps envisioning the invasion of Wall Street by guitar-strumming hippies and dewy-eyed college students.

Just as campus activists played a vital role in the anti-apartheid campaign, students around the world are manning the front lines of the fossil fuel divestment movement. One organization, 350.org, has encouraged organizations controlling more than $5 trillion to commit to full or partial divestment. The group, with more than a million members by the end of 2016, was founded less than ten years earlier by seven students and a teacher—environmentalist and author Bill McKibben—at Vermont's Middlebury College. The number 350 refers to the sustainable level of CO_2 in the atmosphere. It's 400 parts per million now—and growing.

Like the MSCI KLD 400 Social Index, the Fossil Free Indexes make a data-driven case that investors can do good and do well at the same time. To some observers, the idea of fossil-free finance is outrageous; at the end of April 2018, energy stocks made up 6% of the S&P 500 and 20% of the

S&P/TSX Composite, the equivalent Canadian index. Some investors who oppose divestment argue that engagement—ongoing dialogue with corporate management, voting, and similar activities—is more productive. Others feel their responsibility to investors is strictly financial. Some corporations opposing the movement fight back by funding groups that dispute the science of climate change. Disclosure of this spending has become a goal for many ESG investors.

Back in 1970, climate change wasn't even on the radar. Environmentalists worried about nuclear testing, acid rain, and saving the whales. Singers Joni Mitchell, James Taylor, and Phil Ochs performed a benefit concert in Vancouver to raise money for a ragtag crew of activists hoping to buy an old fishing boat, renamed the *Greenpeace*, to sail to Alaska and prevent a nuclear test. The voyage turned into a comedy of errors, put out of its misery early on by the US Navy. "We never quite managed to go in the direction we wanted to go, or be in the place we wanted to be," said one participant. "And we fought bitterly among ourselves about it. Everything we did or said got sucked into an overwhelming power struggle." Nevertheless, their mission made waves globally, attracting media attention and public support, and Greenpeace grew into one of the largest environmental organizations in the world.[21]

Today, environmental campaigns are professionally organized and often global. The September 21, 2014 People's Climate March included events in more than 150 countries, with 400,000 people marching in New York City alone.[22] ESG investors, too, are often members of larger networks, combining forces with like-minded groups. Among the best-known in the US is the Interfaith Center on Corporate Responsibility (ICCR), while the largest global network is UN's Principles for Responsible Investing (UN PRI), with more than a thousand members at the end of April 2017, representing more than $70 trillion in assets under management, all committed to integrating ESG factors into their investment decisions.[23]

Working together, investors of all sizes can change the world. In 2015, as part of an international coalition of fifty-three institutional investors, Frank Coleman's firm filed shareholder resolutions asking BP and Royal Dutch Shell to disclose details of their research into low-carbon energy sources, their climate change policies, and similar information essential to both investment decisions and the public interest. After three hours of discussion, BP shareholders voted 98% in favor of the resolutions.[24] Shell management endured more than four hours of dialogue with concerned shareholders ranging from Greenpeace to a grandmother of seventeen from Alaska who said her kids lived in terror of an oil spill destroying their food supply. The vote came in 99% in favor of adopting the resolutions.[25]

Shareholder engagement topics evolve from year to year. In 2014, creative corporate tax accounting was a new focus for the SRI spotlight. Name-brands including Starbucks, Facebook, and Apple have been accused of paying less than their fair share. At Google's annual meeting, Domini Social Investments (now Domini Impact Investments) and Ethical Funds, a Canadian firm, filed a proposal aimed at drawing attention to Google's practice of reducing its taxes by moving profits through various international hoops "to a mailbox in Bermuda," in the words of one Bloomberg headline. The resolution had no hope of passing without management cooperation, however, due to Google's multi-class voting structure. Class B shares, owned mostly by the founders, commanded ten votes each, while Classes A and C, owned by everyone else, commanded one and zero votes respectively. Not surprisingly, the proposal was voted down. But management did agree to meet with the sponsors of the resolution to discuss the issue.[26] Two years later, Google settled a dispute with UK tax authorities for $185 million, but only after the passage of an anti–tax-avoidance law nicknamed "the Google tax." (The founders reorganized Google in 2015 as part of Alphabet, an umbrella company that includes additional subsidiaries, with the same undemocratic share structure.)

Multi-class voting is controversial. Some argue that management deserves control and can steer a company more smoothly without the risk of takeovers or shareholder impatience. Others, including most corporate governance experts, view investors as part-owners in proportion to the capital they've invested, and therefore one-share-one-vote is the only equitable structure. When Snap Inc., owner of Snapchat, went public in 2017, the company issued zero-voting shares, provoking major index providers to reconsider their positions on this issue. S&P/Dow Jones decided that henceforth, non-voting shares were not welcome in its S&P 500 index. Existing members such as Alphabet could stay, but in the future, companies would have to offer public shareholders equal voting rights if they aspired to be part of this index. Inclusion is not only prestigious but makes a company's shares "must have" purchases for major index funds including the $270 billion SPY.

While anyone with a brokerage account can invest in publicly traded shares, some SRI investments have historically been accessible only to institutions and the mega-wealthy. With the Internet's ability to collapse costs and democratize distribution, new opportunities are opening up. One example is Calvert Foundation's Community Investment Note. Investments of as little as $20 earn a fixed rate of interest while funding organizations around the world devoted to affordable housing, education, microfinance, and similar fields. Calvert Foundation is an offshoot of Calvert Investments, a pioneer in SRI mutual funds. By mid-2017, more than $1.5 billion had been invested, with an investor repayment rate of 100%.[27]

One of Calvert's partners is Shared Interest, a New York–based nonprofit that helps otherwise "un-bankable" South Africans access the capital they need to finance farms and small businesses. Executive director Donna Katzin is another industry pioneer being honored at the SRI Conference this year. Shared Interest's guarantees on more than $20 million of loans have helped more than two million economically marginalized people since the organization began in 1994.

Katzin tells the story of her 2007 visit to a sugar cane co-op in Mpumalanga province, South Africa. She was impressed by the progress the farmers had made developing the bushland they'd been dumped on fifty years earlier by the apartheid government. But as a lender, she had to probe for potential problems. The farmers disclosed a credit risk few investors ever encounter: hungry hippos. Five hippopotamuses living in the nearby Komati River were snacking on the farmers' crops and stunting the growth of young plants with their slobber. Katzin didn't mention exactly how the hippo risk was reduced, but the species is protected, so presumably no hippos were harmed. "And the next growing season, this co-op goes to the bank and gets a loan with no guarantee."

Back in the age of apartheid, Katzin was an advocate of divestment, protesting for US companies to exit South Africa. She tells how, almost thirty years ago, she and scores of others planned a protest at Citibank, the last US bank in the country. It was June 16, 1987, the eleventh anniversary of the Soweto uprising, when hundreds of students protesting peacefully were shot dead in the streets. When Katzin's group contacted National Public Radio hoping for media coverage, NPR declined; anti-apartheid protests just weren't news anymore.

"An hour later the phone rings. We pick it up and it's NPR," she tells us. "The bank has just announced they're pulling out of South Africa." Katzin and hundreds of others headed over to Citibank headquarters on Park Avenue as planned, no longer to protest, however. The event had been transformed into a celebration.

For me, the SRI Conference itself feels like a celebration; more than 600 financial professionals talking about what we can do together to make the world a better place. Despite the sales pitches and glossy brochures in the cavernous exhibit hall, this gathering feels more forthright and friendly, less commercial than other conferences. The program advises us to wear our name badges at all times, but we're also reminded to take care of our bodies ("drink plenty of water... wear comfortable shoes and clothes, and pace yourself") and even to nurture our spirits by relaxing and taking in the starlit skies.

Mindfulness is on the agenda too, with a breakout session called Mindful Finance: For Advisors, Clients, and the Financial Industry. The room fills up and we meditate for a few minutes before hearing personal testimonials from the panelists and a run-down of the research benefits. Mindfulness here includes everything from decades of personal practice to taking a deep breath when you stop at a traffic light. Strictly speaking, though, that too meets MBSR founder Jon Kabat-Zinn's definition: "paying attention in a particular way; on purpose, in the present moment, and non-judgmentally."

Simply paying attention can be a challenge; the non-judgmental aspect—attempting to see the world without labels of good, bad, or neutral—really raises the bar. Like SRI investors, Kabat-Zinn believes drawing attention to what's good for all of us can change the world. In a 2015 German documentary, he spoke about his hope that "businesses could actually re-examine what their ethics are, what kind of added value they contribute to the world, and then align themselves with that." Capitalism, like everything else, continues to evolve. "The real question is, is it evolving in the direction of greed or is it evolving in the direction of wisdom? What is the true business that we are in? Do you want to be in the business of exploitation and harming people but... at such a distance you can sleep at night? Or do you want to actually wake up to the actuality of things and transform it?"[28]

Transforming a world built on speed and greed into one built on compassion and corporate responsibility won't happen overnight, but the influence of SRI investing has been nudging the business world in that direction for decades now.

As I headed home from Colorado Springs, I wondered why I'd never noticed this side of the industry before. How could there be an investment conference this size I'd never heard of, celebrating so many heroes previously unknown to me, folks who'd been fighting the good fight for decades? Of course I'd never noticed them, though. I hadn't been looking.

10

Jumping Off the Bandwagon

"WE ALL HAVE the moves that we do on the dance floor, and it doesn't matter what dance floor we're on, we always fall into those same moves," explains Clare Flynn Levy. "Some of those moves are brilliant. Some of them are ridiculous—if you had a mirror in front of you, you might not make that move."[1]

Flynn Levy coaches investors, rather than dancers, at London-based startup Essentia Analytics. Born in the US, she grew up with a computer in her bedroom. Her familiarity with technology was a competitive advantage when she moved to London in the mid-1990s and joined the investment industry, eventually leading to a position managing a technology fund during the dot-com bubble. Initially, everything she touched turned to gold, but after the bubble burst, nothing seemed to work.[2]

Flynn Levy longed for an app that could track and analyze her investment decisions, "a data-driven feedback loop that could tell me exactly what I was good at, so I could do more of it, and exactly where I was repeatedly destroying value, so I could do less of that," she told HedgeFundsClub.com in 2016. "No one could give me that, and without it, running money felt increasingly futile."[3] At the end of 2009, pregnant with her first child, she laid the plans for Essentia.

While fund companies generate reams of risk metrics and performance data, the focus is on outcomes rather than process. Historically, portfolio managers haven't studied their own play-by-play action the way professional athletes do. Essentia provides the tools for a similar style of training, analyzing individual behavior patterns to identify potential areas of improvement. Holding on to losers is the number one self-destructive habit. "People's behavior when things are going against them is typically not the most rational," says Flynn Levy. We all have logical reasons for why we won't part with our bad investments, but often they're just rationalizations that delay admitting our mistakes. Over-trading is the second most common error. "The fact of the matter," says Flynn Levy, "is that there are portfolio managers—and even more so retail investors—out there who believe that their trading is productive when actually it's the opposite."

When Essentia's software detects a pattern that has detracted from performance in the past, a gentle reminder—which they call a "Nudge"—is sent, not telling the investor what to do, but prompting them to make a deliberate decision at a moment when bias has historically taken hold. "What we've found is that professional investors do make good decisions, on balance, when they are being deliberate about it. But they aren't always being deliberate, left to themselves." Clients receive emails identifying existing positions that look like potential problems. The program can even quantify the cost of ignoring these cues, advising each manager precisely how much value was lost or added as a result of the decision they took in response to the Nudge.

Essentia is typically engaged by investment teams, rather than the risk or compliance departments. The company's consultants build trust by providing confidential individual feedback, allowing clients to be open about any behavior they believe may be impacting their decision-making. Alcohol consumption, for example, can be tracked under an innocuous code name such as "servings of fruit." The goal is to help each money manager improve self-awareness, learning to discern between good instincts and bad habits. "We're the coach who's cheering you on, while holding up a data-centric mirror so that you can be very honest with yourself about what's working and what's not."

Since Essentia was launched in 2014, the service has helped clients improve their performance significantly. Like any training program, however, results depend a great deal on individuals' commitment to changing their behavior. Intellectual honesty is critical, a willingness to look in the mirror and see yourself clearly and admit that your decisions aren't always the wisest. "It seems so obvious," says Flynn Levy, "and yet our instinct is to fight back against anything that doesn't tell us what we want to hear." Essentia's consultants are all ex-fund managers, a fact she feels is essential to the firm's credibility with clients. Also, many are women. "The reason they're not fund managers is that they don't want to be chained to a desk all day long," she tells me. "Being an Essentia Consultant is a very intellectually stimulating option for any ex-portfolio manager who wants more flexibility in their work life. That's not exclusively women, but the lack of flexibility is a major reason that so many women leave the finance industry."

It's unclear whether the dropout rate for female fund managers is higher than for women in other professions, but in terms of gender diversity, the only close comparison seems to be professional wrestling. In the US, women now represent 34% of doctors and 36% of lawyers, but less than 10% of mutual fund managers, a statistic that hasn't budged for more than two decades.[4] Clearly the industry needs more white male MBAs like a fish needs a binomial options pricing model. Yet when I was a fund manager, whenever we recruited, that's mostly who applied. My (all male) colleagues and I aspired to attract a more diverse range of candidates, targeting independent thinkers with nontraditional backgrounds, interests, and skills. Nonetheless, every pool of candidates was depressingly similar.

The best investment team, according to sociologist Brooke Harrington, looks more like the crew of the *Millennium Falcon* from *Star Wars* than the carbon-copy Imperial Stormtroopers. (If you're not familiar with the original film, or need to refresh your memory, crew members included humans Han Solo, Luke Skywalker, and Princess Leia; robots R2-D2 and C-3PO; and Chewbacca, a Wookiee.) "They exhibit diversity by gender, by age, by species, by carbon-based and non-carbon-based life forms, and that's about as diverse as it gets."[5]

Even without robots and an eight-foot-tall fur-covered alien, simply adding a single woman to an all-male crew can improve investment performance. Harrington's 2008 study of US investment clubs found that "groups composed of men and women together earned significantly and consistently higher returns than same-sex groups."[6] Previous studies disagreed on whether diversity within a group was an asset or a liability; sometimes differences drove interpersonal conflict, while other times, they fueled creativity and innovation. Investigating the source of the diversity premium she'd discovered, Harrington found it was informational diversity that helped, not social diversity. Investors using the widest range of information did better, while social differences sometimes caused friction. Other studies have shown that gender-diverse groups have higher "collective intelligence," a sort of group IQ. The best groups at solving challenges weren't those with the smartest members, individually or on average. Instead, social sensitivity, taking turns when talking, and including more women were the keys to success.[7]

Intelligence can actually get in the way, according to Annie Duke, a psychologist, former professional poker player, and author of *Thinking in Bets: Making Smarter Decisions When You Don't Have All the Facts*. Recent research has found that "the smarter you are, the better you are at constructing a narrative that supports your beliefs, rationalizing and framing the data to fit your argument or point of view."[8] In other studies, people with stronger math skills made *more* mistakes than people with weaker math skills when interpreting data related to emotionally charged problems.[9] Somehow, expertise became a handicap.

Duke argues that diversity enhances decision-making, but only when group dynamics support empirical analysis. Otherwise, a group can act like an echo chamber, with members confirming each other's biases and solidifying their shared view as the "right" one. In contrast, a group committed to learning can draw on group wisdom to reveal hidden information and identify the widest range of alternative hypotheses. Furthermore, to open our minds to the full spectrum of potential outcomes, we need to stop looking at decisions as binary yes-or-no choices. "When we move away from a world where there are only two opposing and discrete boxes that decisions can be put in—right or wrong—we start living in the continuum between the extremes."[10]

Just short of earning her PhD in 1992, Duke took a twenty-year detour into the world of professional poker, winning more than $4 million before retiring in 2012. Poker provided a living laboratory of human psychology. Duke discovered she could dramatically improve her performance by adopting an empirical mind-set and viewing errors as learning opportunities rather than writing them off to bad luck.

Asked if she plans to complete her doctorate, Duke assigns a probability of 82%, an answer that reflects her current thinking, and which she can update in either direction over time. "We're addicted to certainty," she tells hosts Jeremy Schwartz of WisdomTree and Wes Gray of Alpha Architect, in an interview for Wharton Business Radio's *Behind the Markets*. By retraining our minds to include the complete continuum between 0 and 100%, we open ourselves to the full range of possible futures. Duke describes herself as an "uncertainty evangelist," saying, "OK! Yay uncertainty! Let's wrap our arms around it, just accept it and start thinking about it in an intentional way that's going to make us all much better decision-makers and more open-minded."

"We can try to control the uncontrollable by looking for security and predictability, always hoping to be comfortable and safe," writes Pema Chödrön, an American Buddhist nun and best-selling author of numerous books, including *Comfortable with Uncertainty: 108 Teachings on Cultivating Fearlessness and Compassion*. "But the truth is that we can never avoid uncertainty. This not-knowing is part of the adventure. It's also what makes us afraid." Cultivating bravery, unfortunately, requires facing our fears. In times of doubt, she suggests asking ourselves, "Do I prefer to grow up and relate to life directly, or do I choose to live and die in fear?"[11]

Both nun and poker champion agree that compassion is another beneficial side effect of remaining open-minded and curious. In a black-or-white world, we see ourselves and others as either winners or losers, with no middle ground. "Euphoria or misery, with no choices in between, is not a very self-compassionate way to live," writes Duke. And by viewing the victories and defeats of others more scientifically, "you come up with more compassionate assessments of other people, where bad things aren't always their fault and good things aren't always luck. You are more likely to walk in their shoes."[12]

Toward the end of her interview on *Behind the Markets*, Gray asks for Duke's hypothesis for why both poker and investing are so male-dominated. She mentions culture and weak mathematics curricula in schools. But she ends by emphasizing the importance of intellectual diversity regardless of gender. "If you have two people who are equally well-informed... and they have opposing viewpoints, generally the truth is going to lie somewhere in the middle."

Focusing on gender alone disregards the full range of possibilities. While past research has suggested that women are better investors than men, the details behind this conclusion are more complex. The famous study "Boys Will Be Boys: Gender, Overconfidence, and Common Stock Investment" found that men hurt their own performance by trading 45% more, and the most active traders reduced their average returns by 7% a year. The authors attributed this result to overconfidence rather than gender: "Both men and women are lousy traders; men merely trade more frequently."[13] Surveys of female amateur investors show they have lower confidence and less experience with investing, which apparently translates into less trading and thus, better results.

Still, the top performers in Brooke Harrington's study were the Asset Accumulators, an all-female group of teachers. For a number of years, they were among the leading investment clubs in the nation. Despite their similar professional backgrounds and lack of gender diversity, the group took an all-business approach to stock picking that ensured productive debate and encouraged dissent. By contrast, the worst performers in Harrington's study were clubs formed through social ties rather than professional or financial ones. Members would support bad investment decisions to preserve friendships, rather than speaking out. Harrington notes that the industry itself has been accused of the same behavior: "Most of the corporate scandals that struck Wall Street during the post-boom era can be traced to business deals embedded in a history of friendship ties among the transaction partners."[14]

While some studies show no difference between male and female professional investors, others suggest that women are less prone to run with the herd.[15] During the dot-com bubble, former Deutsche Bank manager John Coates noticed that his female colleagues on the trading desk were strangely immune to the insanity. "The guys had their eyes rolling back in their heads, desperate to get involved in what some genius was up to, and the women just didn't buy into it."[16] Later, in his second career as a neuroscientist, Coates identified hormones as the culprits: testosterone, which seemed to drive risk-seeking to extremes; and cortisol, which soared with market volatility and seemed to accentuate crashes. Despite the flighty, emotional behavior of Coates's male traders, other studies have shown that male and female fund managers score about even for risk-aversion.

Perhaps my gender protected me from the mass hysteria of the tech wreck, but many male colleagues maintained their composure as well. Being female did provide one memorable advantage, however. I once attended Lucent's annual investor conference, held in an enormous tent outside company headquarters in Murray Hill, New Jersey. After listening all morning to executives sing seductive songs of double-digit sales growth, a crowd of giddy suits rushed to the restrooms. For the first time in my life, I saw women walk right in while the lineup for the men's room ran around the corner.

In the past, however, washrooms were a barrier for women on Wall Street. Muriel Siebert, the first woman to own a seat on the New York Stock Exchange, once threated to have a portable toilet delivered to the seventh floor if a ladies' room wasn't installed there by the end of the year. She'd arrived in New York more than 30 years earlier, in 1954, "with $500, a

Studebaker, and a dream." After proving herself as a star stock analyst, Siebert was unable to convince her employers to pay her the same as her male peers. Frustrated, she started her own firm, Muriel Seibert & Company in 1968. "For 10 years" she recalled, "it was 1,365 men and me."[17]

Siebert was a trailblazer in other ways as well, fighting sexism in Manhattan business clubs, serving as New York state's first female banking superintendent, and negotiating a "no leash, no lease" clause in her no-dogs-allowed office building, a special exemption for Monster Girl, her beloved Chihuahua. Yet Siebert wasn't the first woman stockbroker on Wall Street. In fact, two sisters from Homer, Ohio beat her to it by a hundred years.

Born into poverty to a con man and his religious revivalist wife, sisters Victoria and Tennessee Claflin helped support their family with fortune-telling, faith healing, and communicating with the dead. The Claflins and their seven children travelled across America marketing miracle cures. At age fifteen, Victoria married a doctor, Canning Woodhull, an alcoholic, abuser, and philanderer whom she eventually divorced after eleven years of marriage and two children. Her younger sister, known as Tennie, was charged with manslaughter at age eighteen following the death of a woman her father was treating for breast cancer with a combination of caustic plasters and his daughter's "miracle hands." Neither sister had much in the way of formal education, yet both were brilliant, beautiful, and way before their time.

Bankrolled by Cornelius Vanderbilt, then the richest man in the world, Victoria, thirty-one, and Tennie, twenty-four, opened their own brokerage firm in February 1870. "As their open carriage turned the corner at Wall Street and Broad," writes biographer Myra MacPherson, "the sisters could see the mob moving toward their brand new... firm. Estimates of the crowd reached two thousand and up. One hundred policemen were called out to keep order. Here they were! The first lady stockbrokers in the world!"[18] The sisters impressed onlookers with their speaking skills, business savvy, and shockingly short skirts.

"When I first came to Wall Street," wrote Woodhull, "not 100 women in the whole of the United States owned stocks or dared to show independence in property ownership. Highest positioned men scowled at any thought of woman investment. For a woman to consider a financial question was shuddered over as a profanity."[19]

Despite the Commodore's support and the sisters' reputation for clairvoyance, Woodhull, Claflin & Co. closed after a few years. But by then their attention was focused more on politics than finance. Woodhull became a key player in the US women's suffrage movement, working with Elizabeth Cady Stanton and Susan B. Anthony. In 1872, she ran for US president. Her platform included not only women's rights but an eight-hour workday, welfare for the poor, public education for children, and a repeal of the death penalty. She won few votes, but that was no surprise—many of her supporters were women and thus ineligible to vote.

When women were finally included in political decision-making decades later, we had a profound positive impact on public policy. In the twenty-nine states that granted women the vote over the fifty years prior to the Nineteenth Amendment in 1920, legislators responded to the priorities of their new constituents almost immediately. "Within a single year of suffrage law enactment, patterns of legislative roll call voting shifted dramatically, and local public health spending rose sharply by nearly 45%," a 2007 study reported, estimating that 20,000 children's lives were saved as a result.[20]

Including women can improve not just health, but also wealth. A global survey of almost 22,000 firms in more than 90 countries found that firms with female executives were more profitable than those without.[21] And when analysts at Credit Suisse looked at more than 3,000 public companies in forty countries, they found higher returns on equity, stock valuations, and stock price performance for companies with more women directors and senior executives. These companies also paid higher dividends and suffered significantly fewer cases of bribery, corruption, and fraud.[22]

Gender-lens investing is a category of socially responsible investing that attempts to capture this premium, with products such as Barclays Women in Leadership ETNs (WIL), Pax Ellevate Global Women's Index Fund (PXWEX), and State Street's SPDR SSGA Gender Diversity ETF (SHE). Similar funds trading on Canadian exchanges include Mackenzie Global Leadership Impact ETF (MWMN) and Evolve North American Gender Diversity Index ETF (HERS).

As a mutual fund manager, I never felt my opportunities were limited because I was a woman. Later, however, when I toyed briefly with the idea of starting my own fund, I read the research on the potential barriers. For starters, female entrepreneurs suffer significantly lower access to capital, often resorting to informal forms of financing such as credit cards.[23] In one study, MBA students asked to evaluate investments in fictional initial public offerings (IPOs) were reluctant to back businesses led by women. "Despite identical personal qualifications and firm financials, female Founder/CEOs were perceived as less capable than the male counterparts, and IPOs led by female Founder/CEOs were considered less attractive investments."[24]

Other research has suggested that regardless of performance, male investors prefer male money managers. One study asked students to allocate money to a pair of index funds, virtually identical except that one was managed by the fictional Linda Williams, the other by her almost-identical twin James

Davis. Men demonstrated clear-cut gender bias, allocating 22% less to Linda, while women split their money about 50/50 between the two.[25]

While you might expect investment professionals to be better informed, only about half of CFA Institute members—just 48%—believe diversity improves investment performance. This result was part of an international study conducted in 2016 to better understand the industry's gender imbalance. In consultation with leading finance researchers Renée Adams, Brad Barber, and Terrance Odean (Barber and Odean co-authored the "Boys Will Be Boys" study), the CFA Institute surveyed 135,000 members in more than 150 countries.

The study confirmed that female CFA membership at 18% globally lags well behind female participation in law, medicine, and other professions. But the numbers were strikingly different by country, ranging from 3% in Saudi Arabia to 43% in Vietnam. Only 16% of US members were women, 20% in Canada and the UK. Women members were more achievement-oriented than men, and valued tradition and conformity less. The CFA Institute concluded that the industry might attract more women through greater university outreach and education of investment firms on the benefits of diversity and job flexibility; in other words, public relations.[26]

However, Adams, Barber, and Odean—working with the same data—arrived at a different conclusion: "one avenue to attracting more women to finance would be to structure and reward jobs in a way that supports temporal flexibility," offering more flexible hours and the ability to trade compensation for family time.[27] Their analysis included a factor referred to as "desire to recapture time from work," a measure of respondents' interest in reducing their hours in return for a proportionate reduction in pay; for instance, taking a 10% pay cut in return for working 10% fewer hours. Female CFA members were 75%

more interested than their male peers in earning reduced pay in return for reduced hours. Married women with children were 100% more interested than married men with children.

Flynn Levy believes flex-time might improve not only gender diversity but overall investment performance as well, and that Essentia Analytics' data may someday prove that we think more clearly when we have more downtime. "What if somebody had said to you: 'You make better decisions when you have one day off per week and you work from home and you sleep at least eight hours a night?' If you were a fund manager with actual proof that you perform better when you do things like this, you would give yourself way more permission."

"It's a question of working smarter and then making time for yourself to unwind and spend time with your family, or whatever it is that you do that brings you joy beyond money," Flynn Levy continues. "If you actually have time for that because you know how to work smart, I think your life will be better."

For most of my investment career, my work did bring me joy beyond money. Although my employer was generous with vacation time, I took far less than what was offered. My work seemed to absorb all my time, bleeding over into nights and weekends. There never seemed to be enough hours in the day. Or so it seemed. Maybe I could have done the same job more efficiently with a four-day work week and sleeping more. Maybe busyness was my status symbol.

But even if my rat-race lifestyle was self-imposed, I'm not convinced by the CFA Institute's conclusion that "temporal flexibility in work hours in the investment profession is close to the norm for college-educated workers." This seems to me at odds with not only my own experience but also with the scientists' report. Like the fable of the blind men and the elephant, the truth depends on where we're standing. And the version we believe is often influenced by what Annie Duke calls *motivational reasoning*: we interpret new information in ways that reinforce our pre-existing views, bolstering our certainty rather than challenging our hypotheses. Few people self-identify as blinded by bias, yet research says we all are.

Flynn Levy advises, "If you really want to be good at investing—or anything else for that matter—it's really important to be able to see both your strengths and your weaknesses, and address them." When we're truly honest with ourselves, we'll admit that some of our dance moves are ridiculous, in life and in investing.

When I started meditating, I was a typical female CFA Institute member: achievement-oriented, nontraditional, and nonconformist. I was looking for a quick fix, a productivity hack. Instead, I started to see myself and the world more clearly. Like Flynn Levy's software and Duke's advice on thinking in bets, meditation cultivates awareness of the truth behind our often self-serving but distorted views, helping us differentiate between objective reality and personal beliefs and behavior that may be getting in the way of our own best interests.

I now believe that what Flynn Levy says of Essentia Analytics applies to much more than investing: "At the end of the day it's about being prepared to look in the mirror and look at the truth and learn from it. That's scary but it is entirely doable."

Epilogue

TODAY, MOST OF my money is invested in cheap, plain vanilla index funds. But I also own Alpha Architect's ETFs because Wes Gray and his team are the investors I'd aspire to be if I started over, knowing what I know now about investing and human behavior. I briefly owned an account at a robo-advisor, but my robo-portfolio was so similar to what I was already doing on my own that when I got twelve pages of documentation at tax time, I pulled the plug. That was probably my most dramatic investment move this year. I'm 85% passive, 15% active. And I rarely look at the market.

I returned from the SRI conference ready to change the world, but soon discovered the daunting amount of research required to make sure I was truly aligning my money with my mission. I read a few prospectuses, but no ETF or fund convinced me it was responsible in the ways I care about. And the sustainable energy bonds and community microfinance funds I considered were too risky for my appetite.

That's where I am today. A year from now, who knows? The investment industry is a complex ecology that continues to evolve. Investment products and services forever spawn new mutations both helpful and harmful to consumers. Just when we understand the terms of engagement—active versus passive, commission-based or hourly fees, smart-beta or plain vanilla—someone launches a new innovation that knocks us back into confusion.

What works for me isn't necessarily what's right for you. Personal finance is as much personal as it is financial. Your investment portfolio should be a Rorschach-like reflection of your risk tolerance, time horizon, and personal preferences. Investors have more choices now than ever in history, with something for everyone: traditional mutual funds, do-it-yourself stock picking, robo-advisors, an endless bounty of ETFs. But whatever we own, we should understand what we're paying for—the costs, risks, and expected rewards, including any emotional payoffs. If you haven't read the prospectus, or you don't have a truly trustworthy advisor doing your homework, you're a speculator, not an investor.

When Clare Flynn Levy was asked what individuals could do to improve their investment performance, she recommended keeping a journal, recording decisions in real time, making it impossible to rewrite history later when we know the outcome. It's a low-tech way anyone can learn to make more empirical, less emotional decisions—a free tool almost no one takes advantage of.

Similarly, in fields including investing, medicine, and aeronautics, simple checklists have proven remarkably powerful for reducing errors. Yet checklists are almost universally unpopular. As Dr. Atul Gawande writes in *The Checklist Manifesto*, "We don't like checklists. They can be painstaking. They're not much fun. But I don't think the issue here is mere laziness. There's something deeper, more visceral going on when people walk away not only from saving lives but from making money."[1]

Clearly, the historical view of humans as rational decision makers is at odds with reality. Today, the consensus is turning, with neuroscientists, behavioral economists, and others arguing that we're not only "predictably irrational," but also hardwired for cooperation. Prosocial behavior is biological, driven by chemicals like oxytocin, a hormone associated with empathy, trust, and maternal attachment.[2] Sharing, not selfishness, is human nature, driven by what psychologists call *inequality aversion*, the trait responsible for charitable giving and other "irrational" behavior. When a team of researchers dropped wallets around New York City, about half were mailed back with the money intact.[3]

In recent years, the reputation of the investment industry has risen in the eyes of the public. Yet we still hear more about Wall Street's villains than its heroes—folks like Benjamin Graham, who shared the secrets of successful investing with generations of Columbia University students. And Jack Bogle, who created Vanguard and essentially donated the company to its customers. People like Jon Stein at Betterment, financial planner Sheryl Garrett, Alpha Architect's Wes Gray and his team, and the pioneers of SRI.

The media may focus on the dark side, but there's good news too. Finance, like everything else, is interdependent. Market regulation and consumer protection arise from the ashes of past disasters. Passive investors rely on active investors to keep markets moving. Robo-advisors depend on the availability of ETFs and low-cost computing. ETFs, in turn, depend on low-cost computing plus arbitragers willing to buy and sell baskets of stocks. Momentum investors chase skyrocketing stocks while value investors pan for gold in their wreckage. Computers and humans work better when they work together, and best if you bring a more diverse group of humans to the table—ideally folks with open minds.

The main thing I've learned over the past few years is that nothing is a sure thing; everything changes, often suddenly and surprisingly. The best investment advice I can offer is to embrace uncertainty and try to remain as open-minded as humanly possible. Cultivate "beginner's mind," the view with the fewest firm answers and the broadest bandwidth for learning.

Warren Buffet says investing is simple but not easy. I've heard the same thing said about meditation. Buy what you know. Focus on your breath. You can spend a lifetime practicing either one—or both—and still have plenty to learn. The best strategy, perhaps, is to relax, be curious, and stay open to the full range of possibilities.

Good luck!

Acknowledgments

THIS BOOK BEGAN as a series of essays on a website I built for a hedge fund that never left the launch pad. It evolved into the thesis project for my master's degree, an adventure I could never have completed without the kind cooperation of industry experts including Ric Edelman, Dan Egan, Peter Haynes, Louis Harvey, Matt Hougan, Russ Hill, Antti Petajisto, Clare Flynn Levy, Steve Lockshin, Sheryl Garrett, Wes Gray, Michael Mauboussin, Spencer Sherman, Meir Statman, Jon Stein, and Jason Voss, as well as a few folks who spoke to me for background purposes and wished to remain anonymous. Their stories, as well as their encouragement and generosity with their time, continue to inspire me.

I was welcomed by organizers of two big-ticket industry conferences who graciously granted me media credentials—Jason Lahita of *MarketCounsel Summit 2014* and Vanessa Friedman of *Inside ETFs 2015*—but with no obligation to write positively, or even to write anything at all. Arielle Sobel at Betterment gave me a promotional T-shirt I wear proudly. Otherwise, I received no freebies or preferential treatment.

As every investor should, I verified my subjects' credentials and searched everyone's closet for skeletons, checking out US brokers on BrokerCheck and SEC-registered advisors on the Investment Adviser Public Disclosure (IAPD) website. I read all Forms ADV for the Registered Investment Advisors I interviewed, and the prospectuses of mutual funds and ETFs. I found nothing amiss beyond a couple of financial planners who'd once inadvertently filed papers late in Oregon.

Any errors or omissions are mine alone. And any merit is dedicated to the benefit of all beings. May we all attain omniscience!

Notes

Chapter 1

1 Marjolein 't Hart, Joost Jonker, and Jan Luiten van Zanden, eds., *A Financial History of the Netherlands* (Cambridge: Cambridge University Press, 1997), 53.

2 William Goetzmann and K. Geert Rouwenhorst, "What Is a Long Life Worth?," *Yale Insights*, October 2007.

3 Jan De Vries and Ad van der Woude, *The First Modern Economy: Success, Failure, and Perseverance of the Dutch Economy, 1500–1815* (Cambridge: Cambridge University Press, 1997), 124.

4 K. Geert Rouwenhorst, "The Origin of Mutual Funds," in *The Origins of Value: The Financial Innovations That Created Capital Markets*, ed. William N. Goetzmann and K. Geert Rouwenhorst (Oxford: Oxford University Press, 2005), chapter 15.

5 William N. Goetzmann and K. Geert Rouwenhorst, eds., *The Origins of Value: The Financial Innovations that Created Modern Capital Markets* (Oxford: Oxford University Press, 2005), 257.

6 William N. Goetzmann and K. Geert Rouwenhorst, eds., *The Origins of Value*, 257.

7 This was the motto of the Dutch Republic, also translated as "unity creates strength." In other words, also Eeendragt Maak Magt in Dutch. *Exchange*

History NL, Capital Amsterdam Foundation, accessed July 13, 2018, https://www.beursgeschiedenis.nl/en/moment/the-worlds-first-investment-fund/. Coin information from *Kingdom of Netherlands Trade Ducat, USA Gold*, accessed July 13, 2018, http://www.usagold.com/gold/coins/netherlands-ducat.html.

8 William N. Goetzmann and K. Geert Rouwenhorst, eds., *The Origins of Value*, 261.

9 Marjolein 't Hart, Joost Jonker, and Jan Luiten van Zanden, eds., *A Financial History of the Netherlands*, 57.

10 Rik Frehen, K. Geert Rouwenhorst, and William N. Goetzmann, "Financial Innovation in Late-Eighteenth Century Netherlands: The Case of American Land Securities," (working paper, Yale School of Management, June 5, 2012), 6.

11 David F. Swensen, *Unconventional Success: A Fundamental Approach to Personal Investment* (New York: Free Press, 2005), 122.

12 Investment Company Act of 1940 and Investment Advisers Act of 1940, 76th Cong., 3d Session, Report No. 2639, 6.

13 Michael R. Yogg, *Passion for Reality: The Extraordinary Life of the Investing Pioneer Paul Cabot* (New York: Columbia University Press, 2014), 64–65.

14 *America's First Mutual Fund: A Guide for Long-Term Investors* (Boston: MFS Fund Distributors Inc., 2014); *Treasury Department, United States Internal Revenue Statistics of Income from Returns of Net Income for 1924* (Government Printing Office, Washington DC, 1926). Inflation adjustment from US Inflation Calculator, https://www.usinflationcalculator.com. Average American income at the time is about $52,000 in 2018 dollars.

Chapter 2

1 *Fast Facts* (Canadian Bankers Association, March 2016). Canada dropped to second in 2016, after Finland, and third in 2017, with Finland still in first place, followed by South Africa, according to the *Global Competitiveness Report*, published by the World Economic Forum.

2 John Prestbo, ed., *Ever Wonder How "Blue Chips" Got Their Name?* (Dow Jones Indices, March 12, 2008).

3 Larry Swedroe, "How Not to Create a Fortune," *MoneyWatch*, July 7, 2000.

4 J.D. Coval and T.J. Moskowitz, "Home Bias at Home: Local Equity Preference in Domestic Portfolios," *Journal of Finance* LIV, no. 6 (1999): 2045–2073.

5 Gur Huberman, "Familiarity Breeds Investment," (paper, Columbia University, 1999).

6 David Tuckett and Richard J. Taffler, "Study and Research Methods," in *Fund Management: An Emotional Finance Perspective*, (Charlottesville, VA: The Research Foundation of the CFA Institute, 2012), chapter 2. Only three subjects were women; Tuckett, David, *Minding the Markets: An Emotional Finance View of Financial Instability* (London: Palgrave Macmillan, 2011), 102.

7 David Tuckett, *Minding the Markets*, 158.

8 David Tuckett, *Minding the Markets*, 47–48.

9 *2017 U.S. Investment Company Institute Fact Book: A Review of Trends and Activities in the U.S. Investment Company Industry*, 57th Edition (Washington, DC: Investment Company Institute, 2017), 94.

10 Warren E. Buffett, "The Superinvestors of Graham-and-Doddsville," *Hermes, The Columbia Business School Magazine*, Spring 1984.

11 *Berkshire Hathaway 2013 Annual Report*, at www.BerkshireHathaway.com.

12 Peter L. Bernstein, "Where, Oh Where, are the .400 Hitters of Yesteryear?," *Financial Analysts Journal* (November/December 1998): 6–14.

13 Meir Statman, *What Investors Really Want: Discover What Drives Investor Behavior and Make Smarter Financial Decisions* (New York: McGraw-Hill, 2011), ix.

14 Meir Statman, *What Investors Really Want*, ix.

15 Fischer Black, "Noise," *Journal of Finance* XLI, no. 3 (July 1986): 528–543.

16 Mary-Jane Holmes, "Why Black Swans Create Great Stories," *Every Day Fiction*, December 2014, http://www.everydayfiction.com/flashfictionblog/why-black-swans-create-great-stories/.

17 *Fact Sheet: Black Swans*, Government of Western Australia Swan River Trust, https://www.dpaw.wa.gov.au/.../fact-sheets/Fact%20sheet%20- %20black%20swan.pdf; Black Swan description on the website of New Zealand's Anglers and Hunters for Conservation, 2014; *Australian Dictionary of Biography*, s.v. "Willem de Vlamingh," accessed July 13, 2018 http://adb.anu.edu.au/biography/vlamingh-willem-de-2760.

18 Benoit Mandelbrot and Nassim Nicholas Taleb, "How the Finance Gurus Get Risk All Wrong," *Fortune*, July 11, 2005.

19 Benoit B. Mandelbrot and Richard L. Hudson, *The (Mis)behaviour of Markets: A Fractal View of Risk, Ruin and Reward* (London: Profile Books, 2008), 148–149.

20 Benoit B. Mandelbrot and Richard L. Hudson, *The (Mis)behaviour of Markets*, 95.

21 Benoit B. Mandelbrot and Richard L. Hudson, *The (Mis)behaviour of Markets*, 165.

22 Benoit B. Mandelbrot and Richard L. Hudson, *The (Mis)behaviour of Markets*, 96. The graph of a Gaussian function is the familiar shape known as a bell curve, smooth and symmetrical, nothing like Mandelbrot's cotton prices or Fama's stock prices.

23 Mark Rubinstein, quoted by Jack D. Schwager, *Market Sense and Nonsense: How the Markets Really Work (and How They Don't)* (New York: John Wiley & Sons, 2013), 27.

24 Emanuel Derman, *Models. Behaving. Badly: Why Confusing Illusion with Reality Can Lead to Disaster, on Wall Street and in Life* (New York: Free Press, 2011), 140.

25 Thomas A. Bass, *The Predictors: How a Band of Maverick Physicists Use Chaos Theory to Trade Their Way to a Fortune on Wall Street* (New York: Henry Holt and Company, 1999), 210.

26 From Prediction Company, "Company Profile," www.predict.com.

27 Stephen Batchelor, *Confession of a Buddhist Atheist* (New York: Spiegel & Grau, 2011), 65.

Chapter 3

1 Victor Niederhoffer, *The Education of a Speculator* (New York: John Wiley & Sons, 1997), New York City tennis championship 24, "All gamblers die broke," 173.

2 Victor Niederhoffer, *The Education of a Speculator*, 9.

3 Greg Burns, "'Whatever Voodoo He Uses, It Works': Trader Victor Niederhoffer is as eccentric as he is contrarian," *Business Week*, February 1997.

4 Deepak Gopinath, "The Re-Education of Victor Niederhoffer," *Bloomberg Markets*, July 2006.

5 Deepak Gopinath, "The Re-Education of Victor Niederhoffer," *Bloomberg Markets*, July 2006.

6 Navroz Patel, "The Iconoclast of Brooklyn," *Risk*, March 1, 2004.

7 Michael Ocrant, "Madoff Tops Charts; Skeptics Ask How," *MAR/Hedge* no. 89 (May 2001): 1–5.

8 Victor Niederhoffer, *The Education of a Speculator*, 242.

9 Victor Niederhoffer, *The Education of a Speculator*, 108.

10 Warren E. Buffett, *The Essays of Warren Buffett: Lessons for Corporate America*, 1st rev. ed., compiled by Lawrence Cunningham, (Cunningham Group, 2001), 35; Graham, Benjamin, *The Intelligent Investor: The Classic Bestseller on Value Investing* (New York: HarperCollins, 1973), xv.

11 Benjamin Graham, *The Intelligent Investor*, vii.

12 Warren E. Buffett, "The Superinvestors of Graham-and-Doddsville," *Hermes, The Columbia Business School Magazine*, Spring 1984.

13 Benjamin Graham, *Memoirs of the Dean of Wall Street* (New York: McGraw-Hill, 1996), 142.

14 Joe Carlen, *The Einstein of Money: The Life and Timeless Financial Wisdom of Benjamin Graham* (Amherst, NY: Prometheus Books, 2012), 237, 301–302.

15 Benjamin Graham, *The Intelligent Investor*, 1, 3.

16 Justin Kruger and David Dunning, "Unskilled and Unaware of It: How Difficulties in Recognizing One's Own Incompetence Lead to Inflated Self-Assessments," *Journal of Personality and Social Psychology* 77, no. 6 (1999): 1121–1134.

17 Benjamin Graham, *Memoirs of the Dean of Wall Street*, 87.

18 Benjamin Graham, *Memoirs of the Dean of Wall Street*, 113.

19 Benjamin Graham, *Memoirs of the Dean of Wall Street*, 92.

20 Benjamin Graham, *The Intelligent Investor*, 94.

21 John Quirt, "Benjamin Graham: The Grandfather of Investment Value," in *The Rediscovered Benjamin Graham: Selected Writings for the Wall Street Legend*, ed. Janet Lowe (New York: John Wiley & Sons, 1999), 252.

22 Richard Read, "Midlife Crisis Cars: Men Want Black & Sporty, Women Want Red & Practical," *TheCarConnection.com*, February 4, 2015.

23 Brooke Harrington, *Pop Finance: Investment Clubs and the New Investment Populism* (Princeton: Princeton University Press, 2008), 155, 165.

24 Warren E. Buffett, *The Essays of Warren Buffett*, 80.

25 Jason M. Breslow, "John Bogle: The 'Train Wreck' Awaiting American Retirement," *Frontline*, April 23, 2013, https://www.pbs.org/wgbh/frontline/article/john-bogle-the-train-wreck-awaiting-american-retirement/.

26 Dan Ariely, *Predictably Irrational: The Hidden Forces that Shape our Decisions*, Revised and Expanded Edition (New York: Harper Perennial 2009), 120.

27 Dan Ariely, *Predictably Irrational*, 136.

28 Richard H. Thaler and Cass R. Sunstein, *Nudge: Improving Decisions about Health, Wealth, and Happiness*, rev. ed. (New York: Penguin Books, 2009), 42.

29 Warren E. Buffett, *The Essays of Warren Buffett*, 81.

Chapter 4

1 Stephen Batchelor, "A Secular Buddhism," *Journal of Global Buddhism* 13 (2012): 87–107, 88; and Stephen Batchelor and Pat Rockman, "A Tale of Two Mindfulnesses," *MikeHoolboom.com*, May 2011, http://mikehoolboom.com/?p=11850.

2 Chögyam Trungpa, *Glimpses of Abhidharma: From a Seminar on Buddhist Psychology* (Boston: Shambhala Publications Inc., 2001), 59.

3 Kathryn Schulz, *Being Wrong: Adventures in the Margin of Error* (New York: HarperCollins, 2010), 18.

4 His Holiness the Dalai Lama, *Dzogchen: The Heart Essence of the Great Perfection* (Ithaca, NY and Boulder, CO: Snow Lion Publications, 2000), 35.

5 George Kinder, *The Seven Stages of Money Maturity: Understanding the Spirit and Value of Money in Your Life* (New York: Dell Publishing, 1999), 284.

6 Vincent Horn, "The Dark Side of Dharma," *Buddhist Geeks* (podcast), September 2011.

7 Willoughby Britton's presentation to the Dalai Lama at Mind and Life XXIV—Latest Findings in Contemplative Science, April 24, 2012, accessed March 18, 2016, https://vimeo.com/67777082.

8 Joe Pinsker, "Corporations' Newest Productivity Hack: Meditation," *The Atlantic*, March 10, 2015.

9 Madhav Goyal, MD, MPH; Sonal Singh, MD, MPH; Erica M.S. Sibinga, MD, MHS; Neda F. Gould, PhD; Anastasia Rowland-Seymour, MD; Ritu Sharma,

BSc; Zackary Berger, MD, PhD; Dana Sleicher, MS, MPH; David D. Maron, MHS; Hasan M. Shihab, MBChB, MPH; Padmini D. Ranasinghe, MD, MPH; Shauna Linn, BA; Shonali Saha, MD; Eric B. Bass, MD, MPH; and Jennifer A. Haythornthwaite, PhD, "Meditation Programs for Psychological Stress and Well-Being: A Systematic Review and Meta-Analysis," *JAMA Internal Medicine* 174, no. 3 (2014): 357–368.

Chapter 5

1 Wesley R. Gray, *Embedded: A Marine Corps Adviser Inside the Iraqi Army* (Annapolis, MD: Naval Institute Press, 2009), 58.

2 Wesley R. Gray, *Embedded*, 64.

3 Phil Primack, "Fama's Market," *Tufts Magazine*, Winter 2014.

4 Eugene Fama, "My Life in Finance," *Annual Review of Financial Economics* 3 (December 2011): 1–15.

5 Wesley R. Gray, PhD, and David P. Foulke, "A Framework for Assessing Investment Strategies: Stick to the FACTS," *Alpha Architect*, September 16, 2014, https://alphaarchitect.com/2014/09/16/a-framework-for-investment-manager-selection-stick-to-the-facts/.

6 Ben Carlson, "Q&A with Alpha Architect's Wes Gray: Part II," A Wealth of Common Sense (blog), November 24, 2014, http://awealthofcommonsense.com/2014/11/qa-alpha-architects-wes-gray-part-ii/.

7 Roger Lowenstein, "Long-Term Capital Management: It's a Short-Term Memory," *New York Times*, September 7, 2008.

8 James Montier, *Behavioural Investing: A Practitioner's Guide to Applying Behavioural Finance* (New York: John Wiley & Sons, 2007), 118.

9 Andrea Frazzini, David Kabiller, and Lasse Heje Pedersen, "Buffett's Alpha" (National Bureau of Economic Research working paper, November 21, 2013).

10 Ron Lieber, "Finding Success, Passionate Followers in Tow," *New York Times*, January 29, 2011.

11 Emily Zulz, "Top 10 Mutual Fund Firms Most Trusted by Advisors: Cogent," *ThinkAdvisor.com*, July 23, 2015, https://www.thinkadvisor.com/2015/07/23/top-10-mutual-fund-firms-most-trusted-by-advisors/?slreturn=20180613190350.

12 Susan Gittins, "Index Participation Units May Hammer Equity Funds," *Financial Post*, March 13, 1990.

13 $248 million Canada dollars, converted at 0.847488, the March 1990 Canadian/US exchange rate according to OFX, http://www.canadianforex.ca/forex-tools/historical-rate-tools/monthly-average-rates.

14 Dennis Slocum, "TSE Members Cool Toward TIPs," *Globe and Mail*, February 14, 1990.

15 Jade Hemeon, "Popular TIPs Units Get Fourth Reissue," *Toronto Star*, September 24, 1991.

16 State Street Global Advisors, "SPY: The Idea That Spawned an Industry," Filed Pursuant to Rule 433, Registration No. 333-180974, January 25, 2013.

17 Kathleen Pender, "Nathan Most, Creator of Exchange-Traded Funds, Still a Visionary," *SFGate.com*, July 18, 2000, https://www.sfgate.com/business/networth/article/Nathan-Most-Creator-of-Exchange-Traded-Funds-2713311.php.

18 ETF statistics from press release "ETFs/ETPs Listed Globally Have Gathered a Record 372.0 Billion US Dollars in Net New Assets in 2015, According to ETFGI" (London: ETFGI, January 11, 2016).

19 Joanne M. Hill, Dave Nadig, and Matt Hougan, *A Comprehensive Guide to Exchange-Traded Funds (ETFs)* (Charlottesville, VA: CFA Institute Research Foundation, 2015), 7.

20 *A Global Guide to Strategic Beta Exchange-Traded Products* (Morningstar Manager Research, September 2017).

21 Abhishek Gupta and Raman Aylur Subramanian, *The MSCI Quality Mix Index: Combining the MSCI Quality, Value and Low Volatility Factor Indexes* (MSCI Index Applied Research, May 2014).

22 Peter L. Bernstein, *Capital Ideas: The Improbable Origins of Modern Wall Street* (New York: The Free Press, 1992), 233–252; Ancell, Kate, "The Origin of the Index Fund," University of Chicago Booth School of Business, March 28, 2012.

23 Denys Glushkov, "How Smart Are Smart Beta Exchange-Traded Funds? Analysis of Relative Performance and Factor Exposure," *Journal of Investment Consulting* 17 no. 1 (2016): 50–74.

24 Denys Glushkov, "How Smart Are Smart Beta ETFs?"

25 Garry Kasparov, "The Chess Master and the Computer," *The New Yorker*, February 11, 2010.

26 Garry Kasparov, *How Life Imitates Chess: Making the Right Moves—From the Board to the Boardroom* (New York: Bloomsbury, 2007), 4.

27 D.T. Max, "The Prince's Gambit," *The New Yorker*, March 21, 2011.

28 Nigel Farndale, "Game Face," *The Daily Telegraph*, November 28, 2015; D.T. Max, "The Prince's Gambit."

29 "NRK TV Spectacular: Carlsen vs Norway, Frederic Friedel," *Chess News*, December 1, 2014, http://en.chessbase.com/post/nrk-tv-spectacular-carlsen-vs-norway.

30 "Nudge Nudge, Think Think: The Use of Behavioural Economics in Public Policy Shows Promise," *The Economist*, March 24, 2012.

31 Ryan Lizza, "Inside the Crisis: Larry Summers and the White House Economic Team," *The New Yorker*, October 12, 2009.

32 Bradford Cornell, "What Moves Stock Prices: Another Look," *Journal of Portfolio Management* (Spring 2013): 32–38.

33 Ben Carlson, "Q&A with Alpha Architect's Wes Gray: Part II."

Chapter 6

1 Numbers from Michael Arrington, "*The TechCrunch Disrupt Final Five: Betterment, MOVIECLIPS, Publish2, Soluto and UJAM*," *TechCrunch.com*, May 26, 2010, https://techcrunch.com/2010/05/26/the-techcrunch-disrupt-final-five-betterment-movieclips-publish2-soluto-and-ujam/.

2 Charles Merrill on his fascination with chain stores, as quoted in Winthrop H. Smith Jr., *Catching Lightning in a Bottle: How Merrill Lynch Revolutionized the Financial World* (New York: John Wiley & Sons, 2013), 35.

3 Winthrop H. Smith Jr., *Catching Lightning in a Bottle*, 557.

4 Winthrop H. Smith Jr., *Catching Lightning in a Bottle*, 487.

5 Christopher Gray, "When a Monster Plied the West Side," *New York Times*, December 22, 2011; David W. Dunlap, "Elevated Freight Line Being Razed Amid Protests," *New York Times*, January 15, 1991.

6 M.G. Siegler, "And The Winner Of TechCrunch Disrupt Is... Soluto!," *TechCrunch.com*, May 26, 2010, https://techcrunch.com/2010/05/26/techcrunch-disrupt-winner-soluto/.

7 Michael Arrington, "Unveiled: The TechCrunch Disrupt Cup," *TechCrunch.com*, May 23, 2010, https://techcrunch.com/2010/05/23/unveiled-the-techcrunch-disrupt-cup/.

8 $640,000 number is from Ronny Kerr, "When Betterment Was Young: The Early Years," *Vator*, December 2, 2018, http://vator.tv/news/2016-12-02-when-betterment-was-young-the-early-years.

9 Interview with Jon Stein, February 5, 2015.

10 Robin D. Schatz, "How We Got Funded: Betterment," *Inc.com*, March 6, 2013.

11 Chris Sacca, "About Me," What Is Left (blog), http://www.whatisleft.org/about.html.

12 Interview with Jon Stein, January 16, 2015.

13 Suzanne Duncan, Daniel W. Latimore, and Shankar Ramamurthy, *Toward Transparency and Sustainability: Building a New Financial Order*, (Somers, NY: IBM Institute for Business Value, 2009), 1.

14 Suzanne Duncan, Daniel W. Latimore, and Shankar Ramamurthy, *Toward Transparency and Sustainability*, 12.

15 Suzanne Duncan, Daniel W. Latimore, and Shankar Ramamurthy, *Toward Transparency and Sustainability*, 8.

16 Francis M. Kinniry, Jr., Colleen M. Jaconetti, Michael DiJoseph, and Yan Zilbering, *Putting a Value on Your Value: Quantifying Vanguard Advisor's Alpha*, (Valley Forge, PA: The Vanguard Group, March 2014).

17 John Harvard's Journal, "'Sex' without DeVore," *Harvard Magazine*, January–February 2001; Bryan Marquard, "Irven DeVore, Celebrated Harvard Anthropologist, Dies at 79," *Boston Globe*, September 9, 2014.

18 Panic architecture definition and Facebook example from *CyborgAnthropology.com*, accessed July 14, 2018, http://cyborganthropology.com/Panic_Architecture.

19 Stephen Mitchell, *Tao Te Ching: A New English Version* (New York: Harper Perennial, 1991), chapter 60.

20 Philip K. Dick, *Do Androids Dream of Electric Sheep?* (New York: Doubleday, 1968).

21 "Do Androids Dream of Electric Sheep?/Blade Runner (1968)," *The Philip K. Dick Bookshelf*, accessed July 14, 2018, http://www.pkdickbooks.com/SFnovels/Do_Androids_Dream.php. According to *The Philip K. Dick Bookshelf*, the movie *Blade Runner* was set in 2021, so later editions of *Do Androids Dream of Electric Sheep?* updated the setting from 1992 to be consistent.

22 Interview with Jon Stein, January 16, 2015.

23 Burton Malkiel, *A Random Walk Down Wall Street: The Time-Tested Strategy for Successful Investing* (New York: W.W. Norton & Company, 2012), 203–205.

24 Jason Kincaid, "Betterment Wants to Be Your New Savings Account," May 24, 2010, https://techcrunch.com/2010/05/24/betterment-wants-to-be-your-new-savings-account/.

25 *Reshaping around the Investor: Global ETF Research 2017* (London: EY, 2017), 13.

26 W. Brian Arthur, *The Nature of Technology: What It Is and How It Evolves* (New York: Free Press, 2009), 149.

27 W. Brian Arthur, *The Nature of Technology*, 152.

28 The history of Bessemer Venture Partners, according to their website at http://www.bvp.com/about/history.

29 Jon Stein, "Betterment Raises Another $60 Million for Smarter Investing," February 19, 2015, https://www.betterment.com/resources/betterment-raises-another-60-million-for-smarter-investing/.

30 Beth Potier, "They've Got Personality... Times Ten: Dunster House Suitemates Share an Intimate Look at One Another," *Harvard University Gazette*, June 7, 2001.

31 Interview with Jon Stein, January 16, 2015.

Chapter 7

1 Barack Obama, "Remarks by the President at the AARP" (speech at AARP, Washington, DC, February 23, 2015), https://obamawhitehouse.archives.gov/the-press-office/2015/02/23/remarks-president-aarp.

2 Interview with Sheryl Garrett, July 14, 2015.

3 US Securities and Exchange Commission, *SEC Warns of Purported Financial Professionals Using False Credentials to Attract Investors* (US Securities and Exchange Commission press release, 2015-108), https://www.sec.gov/news/pressrelease/2015-108.html.

4 *Affluence in America; A Financial View of the Mass Affluent* (Nielsen Company, 2017), 2.

5 Michael S. Finke and Thomas Patrick Langdon, "The Impact of the Broker-Dealer Fiduciary Standard on Financial Advice" (paper, March 9, 2012), 1.

6 Halah Touryalai, "BofA Has a Good Idea: Tells Merrill to Drop Small Clients," *Forbes.com*, January 6, 2012, https://www.forbes.com/sites/halahtouryalai/2012/01/06/bofa-has-a-good-idea-tells-merrill-lynch-to-drop-small-clients/#8764a72edc93.

7 Winthrop H. Smith Jr., *Catching Lightening in a Bottle: How Merrill Lynch Revolutionized the Financial World* (New York: John Wiley & Sons, 2013), 192–193.

8 Winthrop H. Smith Jr., *Catching Lightening in a Bottle*, 200.

9 Rudy Mezzetta, "CRM2 Is Having an Impact," *Investment Executive*, December 1, 2017, https://www.investmentexecutive.com/in-depth_/special-reports/crm2-disclosure-is-having-an-impact/.

10 Meir Statman, "Investors Want Help, But Many Lack Trust," *Investment News*, December 5, 2010.

11 Pablo S. Torre, "How (and Why) Athletes Go Broke," *Sports Illustrated*, March 23, 2009.

12 Lisa Shidler, "How Brian Hamburger Won Speaking Commitments from Mark Cuban, Sallie Krawcheck and Eliot Spitzer without Throwing Money at the Challenge," RIABiz.com, June 12, 2014, https://riabiz.com/a/2014/6/12/how-brian-hamburger-won-speaking-commitments-from-mark-cuban-sallie-krawcheck-and-eliot-spitzer-without-throwing-money-at-the-challenge.

13 *U.S. Investors and the Fiduciary Standard: A National Opinion Survey* (ORC/Infogroup, September 15, 2010).

14 Robert B. Cialdini, PhD, *Influence: The Psychology of Persuasion* (New York: Collins Business, 2007), 227.

15 Henry Blodget, *The Wall Street Self-Defense Manual: A Consumer's Guide to Intelligent Investing* (Atlas Books, 2007), U.S. Open tickets 113, Vanguard 111.

16 Eliot Spitzer, *Protecting Capitalism: Case by Case* (New York: Rosetta Books, 2013), 52–53.

17 Martin Wheatley, "Making Innovation Work for Firms and Consumers" (speech by Chief Executive, Financial Conduct Authority, London, May 29, 2014).

18 Matthew R. Morey, "The Kiss of Death: A 5-star Morningstar Mutual Fund Rating?" (paper, Pace University, September 2003).

19 Del Guercio and Tkac (2002), cited in Matthew R. Morey, "The Kiss of Death."

20 Jeffrey Ptak, CFA, "Report Card: How Well Has the Morningstar Analyst Rating Performed?," *Morningstar.com*, December 18, 2017, https://www.morningstar.com/articles/840926/report-card-how-well-has-the-morningstar-analyst-r.html.

21 Sunita Sah, George Loewenstein, and Daylian M. Cain, "The Burden of Disclosure: Increased Compliance with Distrusted Advice," *Journal of Personality and Social Psychology* 104, no. 2 (2013): 289–304.

22 Uwe Dulleck, Rudolf Kerschbamer, and Matthias Sutter, "The Economics of Credence Goods: An Experiment on the Role of Liability, Verifiability, Reputation, and Competition," *American Economic Review* 101, no. 2 (2011): 526–555.

23 *The Forgotten Investor* (Boston: State Street Center for Applied Research, 2014).

Chapter 8

1 Phil Ashburn, *Ashburn Fiduciary Statement*, delivered at the Forum on Ending the Retirement Savings Drain, available on YouTube: "Cummings & Warren to Hold Forum: 'Ending the Retirement Savings Drain & Improving Economic Security,'" March 24, 2015, https://www.youtube.com/watch?v=nGyCW3csAyE.

2 Phil Ashburn, *Ashburn Fiduciary Statement.*

3 Tara Siegel Bernard, "Taking a Broker to Arbitration," *New York Times*, July 18, 2014.

4 Data from "Household Data Annual Averages, Employment Status of the Civilian Noninstitutional Population by Age, Sex, and Race, 2017," the United States Department of Labor, Bureau of Labor Statistics, accessed March 26, 2018, https://www.bls.gov/cps/cpsaat03.htm.

5 *A "Snapshot,"* Social Security Administration, July 2017, https://www.ssa.gov/pubs/EN-05-10006.pdf.

6 "Canada Pension Plan Enhancement: Effects on CPP Retirement Pension and Post-retirement Benefit" *Canada.ca*, last modified April 11, 2017, https://www.canada.ca/en/services/benefits/publicpensions/cpp/cpp-enhancement.html.

7 Javier Escamilla, "The Social Security Dilemma" (paper, Ethics of Development in Global Environment [EDGE]), accessed November 14, 2015, https://web.stanford.edu/class/e297c/poverty_prejudice/soc_sec/hsocialsec.htm.

8 John C. Bogle, *The Man in the Arena: Panel Discussion of the John C. Bogle Legacy Book* (New York: December 5, 2013), 5.

9 John C. Bogle, *The Journal of Portfolio Management and John C. Bogle: A Four Decade Relationship* (Valley Forge, PA: Vanguard, 2014), 139.

10 John C. Bogle, *The Journal of Portfolio Management and John C. Bogle*, 141.

11 Lewis Braham, *The House That Bogle Built: How John Bogle and Vanguard Reinvented the Mutual Fund Industry* (New York: McGraw-Hill, 2011), 37.

12 Lewis Braham, *The House That Bogle Built*, 241.

13 Eric Kingson and Monique Morrissey, "Can Workers Offset Social Security Cuts by Working Longer?" (Economic Policy Institute Briefing Paper #343, Economic Policy Institute, May 30, 2012).

14 Susan Rosegrant, "The New Retirement: No Retirement?" in *ISR Sampler*, (Ann Arbor: Institute for Social Research, University of Michigan, Spring 2013), 5, accessed July 14, 2018, home.isr.umich.edu/files/2013/05/ISR-Sampler_Spring-13_web.pdf.

15 *Understanding the Benefits 2015*, Social Security Administration.

16 *When to Start Receiving Retirement Benefits*, Society Security Administration, August 2015.

17 Charles D. Ellis, Alicia H. Munnell, and Andrew D. Eschtruth, *Falling Short: The Coming Retirement Crisis and What to Do about It* (Oxford: Oxford University Press, 2014), 102.

18 John C. Bogle, "Lightning Strikes: The Creation of Vanguard, the First Index Mutual Fund, and the Revolution It Spawned," *The Journal of Portfolio Management*, Special 40th Anniversary Issue (2014), 45.

19 John C. Bogle, *Don't Count on It! Reflections on Investment Illusions, Capitalism, "Mutual" Funds, Indexing, Entrepreneurship, Idealism, and Heroes* (New York: John Wiley & Sons, 2011), 376.

20 Lewis Braham, *The House That Bogle Built*, 193.

21 Bill Bernstein, "The Bogle Impact: A Roundtable," *Journal of Indexes* (March/April 2012), 25.

22 Michael Finke, PhD, CFP; Wade D. Pfau PhD, CFP; and David M. Blanchett CFA, CFP, "The 4% Rule is Not Safe in a Low-Yield World" (paper, January 15, 2013).

23 Bill Bengen, "How Much is Enough?" *Financial Adviser*, May 1, 2012.

24 Kathleen D. Voss and Roy F. Baumeister, "Can Satisfaction Reinforce Wanting? A New Theory About Long-Term Changes in Strength of Motivation," in *Handbook of Motivation Science*, eds. James Y. Shah and Wendi L. Gardner (New York: Guilford Press, 2008), 373–389.

25 Dzigar Kongtrül, *It's Up to You: The Practice of Self-Reflection on the Buddhist Path* (Boston: Shambhala Publications, 2006), 70.

26 Nagarjuna, *Nagarjuna's Letter to a Friend*, trans. Dr. Alexander Berzin, accessed July 14, 2018, https://studybuddhism.com/en/tibetan-buddhism/original-texts/sutra-texts/letter-to-a-friend.

27 Lalin Anik, Lara B. Aknin, Michael I. Norton, and Elizabeth W. Dunn, "Feeling Good about Giving: The Benefits (and Costs) of Self-Interested Charitable Behavior" (Working Paper 10-012, Harvard Business School, 2009).

28 Silvia Bellezza, Anat Keinan, and Neeru Paharia, "Conspicuous Consumption of Time: When Busyness and Lack of Leisure Time Become a Status Symbol," *Journal of Consumer Research* 44, no. 1, (June 1, 2017): 118–138.

29 Valerie Wilson and Janelle Jones, *Working Harder or Finding It Harder to Work: Demographic Trends in Annual Work Hours Show an Increasingly Fractured Workforce* (Washington, DC: Economic Policy Institute, February 22, 2018).

30 Wilkinson, Richard and Kate Pickett, *The Spirit Level: Why Greater Equality Makes Societies Stronger* (New York: Bloomsbury, 2009), 178.

Chapter 9

1 Paul K. Piff, Pia Deitze, Matthew Feinberg, Daniel M. Stancato, and Dacher Keltner, "Awe, the Small Self, and Prosocial Behavior," *Journal of Personality and Social Psychology* 108, no. 6 (2015): 883–899.

2 *Catholic Investment Screening*, Christian Brothers Investment Services, Inc., April 2015.

3 *CBIS & Catholic Responsible Investing*, Christian Brothers Investment Services, Inc., December 2015.

4 "Where Do We Go from Here?", in *A Call to Conscience: The Landmark Speeches of Dr. Martin Luther King, Jr.*, eds. Clayborne Carson and Kris Shepard (New York: Intellectual Properties Management with Grand Central Publishing, 2002), 176.

5 Amy Domini, *Socially Responsible Investing: Making a Difference and Making Money* (Chicago: Dearborn Trade, 2001), 35.

6 *Academic and Market Research on Divestment* (New York: Pension Consulting Alliance, May 2014).

7 Siew Hong Teoh, Ivo Welch, and C. Paul Wazzan, "The Effect of Socially Activist Investment Policies on the Financial Markets: Evidence from the South African Boycott" (UCLA Working Paper 16-94, March 27, 1998).

8 Amy Domini, *Socially Responsible Investing*, 35.

9 *Report on US Sustainable, Responsible, and Impact Investing Trends 2016*, US SIF Foundation, The Forum for Sustainable and Responsible Investment.

10 *Report on US Sustainable, Responsible, and Impact Investing Trends 2016*, US SIF Foundation, The Forum for Sustainable and Responsible Investment.

11 Jad Mouawad, "For BP, a History of Spills and Safety Lapses," *New York Times*, May 8, 2010.

12 Mark Carney, "Inclusive Capitalism: Creating a Sense of the Systemic" (speech to the Conference on Inclusive Capitalism, May 27, 2014).

13 Robert C. Solomon, "Free Enterprise, Sympathy, and Virtue," in *Moral Markets: The Critical Role of Values in the Economy*, ed. Paul J. Zak (Princeton: Princeton University Press, 2008), 35–36.

14 John Wesley, "The Use of Money" (sermon), accessed March 18, 2016, http://www.umcmission.org/Find-Resources/John-Wesley-Sermons/Sermon-50-The-Use-of-Money.

15 Amy Domini, "Speech at Dartmouth-Hitchcock Medical," (September 25, 2009), accessed March 2016, https://www.domini.com/why-domini/domini-insights/speeches-interviews/amy-domini-speech-dartmouth-hitchcock-medical.

16 Gunnar Friede, Timo Busch, and Alexander Bassen, "ESG and Financial Performance: Aggregated Evidence from More than 2,000 Empirical Studies," *Journal of Sustainable Finance & Investment* 5, no. 4 (2015): 210–233; and "Sustainable Reality: Understanding the Performance of Sustainable Investment Strategies" (Morgan Stanley Institute for Sustainable Investing, 2015).

17 Rudy Ruitenberg, "Merlot Wines Under Threat as Bordeaux Hit by Rising Temperatures," *Bloomberg News*, October 22, 2015.

18 Oliver Nieburg, "Mars, Nestlé and Hershey Face Fresh Cocoa Child Labor Class Action Lawsuits," *Confectionery News*, September 30, 2015.

19 Information on the Deepwater Horizon Oil Spill from Richard Pallardy, "Deepwater Horizon oil spill of 2010," *Brittanica.com*, last modified April 13, 2018, https://www.britannica.com/event/Deepwater-Horizon-oil-spill-of-2010.

20 *A Legal Framework for the Integration of Environmental, Social, and Governance Issues into Institutional Investment* (produced by Freshfields Bruckhaus Deringer for the Asset Management Working Group of the UNEP Finance Initiative, October 2005).

21 Information on Greenpeace's history from Greenpeace website, accessed March 5, 2016, http://www.greenpeace.org/canada/en/About-us/History/.

22 "Largest Global Call for Climate Action in History: Nearly 400,000 march in NY, events in over 150 countries," *PeoplesClimate.com*, accessed March 2016, http://2014.peoplesclimate.org/press-release/largest-global-call-for-climate-action-in-history/.

23 PRI Reporting Framework 2017: Snapshot Report, *UNPRI.org*, accessed July 15, 2018, https://app.powerbi.com/view?r=eyJrIjoiZjA2OTA5MWUtMzc4OC00MTZhLWIyZDYtYTc3NDMzOGE1OGFjIiwidCI6ImZiYzI1NzBkLWE5OGYtNDFmMS1hOGFkLTEyYjEzMWJkOTNlOCIsImMiOjh9.

24 Terry Macalister, BP Promises More Transparency on Climate Change Issues," *The Guardian*, April 16, 2015, http://www.theguardian.com/business/2015/apr/16/bp-promises-more-transparency-on-climate-issues.

25 Sean Farrel, "Climate Change Dominates Marathon Shell Annual General Meeting," *The Guardian*, May 19, 2015, http://www.theguardian.com/business/2015/may/19/climate-change-shell-annual-meeting-oil-global-warming-resolution-shareholders.

26 "Google AGM: If At First You Don't Succeed, Try, Try Again," *EthicalFunds.com* (newsletter), June 2014, https://www.ethicalfunds.com/en/newsletter-june-2014/.

27 Community Investment Note Fact Sheet (Bethesda, MD: Calvert Impact Capital, June 2017).

28 Samuel Stefan and Nick Oakley, *The Mindfulness Revolution* (Burgstrasse, Switzerland: Arthio Productions, July 2015).

Chapter 10

1 "Behavioural Investing: Interview with Clare Flynn Levy, Essentia Analytics," by Tamzin Freeman, *Piworld.co.uk*, December 21, 2017, https://www.youtube.com/watch?v=vfg6k_k4Bjw.

2 Interview with Clare Flynn Levy, January 2, 2015.

3 "Clare Flynn Levy: Making Fund Managers Better with Behavioural Data Analytics," *HedgeFundsClub.com*, July 2016, at http://www.hedgefundsclub.com/archives/4006.

4 "Professionally Active Physicians by Gender," Henry J. Kaiser Family Foundation, data for March 2018, accessed July 15, 2018, https://www.kff.org/other/state-indicator/physicians-by-gender/?currentTimeframe=0&sortModel=%7B%22colId%22:%22Location%22,%22sort%22:%22asc%22%7D; *A Current Glance at Women in the Law*, American Bar Association, 2017; and *Fund Managers by Gender* (Morningstar, June 2015).

5 Brooke Harrington, "Dollars and Difference: Task Commitment, Diversity, and Workgroup Outcomes," speech at Credit Suisse First Boston Thought Leader Forum 2003, accessed March 18, 2016, http://www.csfb.com/thoughtleaderforum/2003/harrington_sidecolumn.shtml (page discontinued).

6 Brooke Harrington, *Pop Finance: Investment Clubs and the New Investor Populism* (Princeton: Princeton University Press, 2008), 83.

7 Anita Williams Woolley, Christopher F. Chabris, Alex Pentland, Nada Hasmi, and Thomas W. Malone, "Evidence for a Collective Intelligence Factor in the Performance of Human Groups," *Science*, October 29, 2010.

8 Annie Duke, *Thinking in Bets: Making Smarter Decisions When You Don't Have All the Facts* (New York: Portfolio 2018), 62.

9 Annie Duke, *Thinking in Bets*, 64.

10 Annie Duke, *Thinking in Bets*, 34.

11 Pema Chödrön, *Comfortable with Uncertainty: 108 Teachings on Cultivating Fearlessness and Compassion* (Boston: Shambhala Publications Inc., 2003), 5–6.

12 Annie Duke, *Thinking in Bets*, 114.

13 Brad M. Barber and Terrance Odean, "Research Summary: Why Do Investors Trade Too Much?" (paper, UC Davis Graduate School of Management, University of California, 2006).

14 Brooke Harrington, *Pop Finance: Investment Clubs and the New Investor Populism* (Princeton: Princeton University Press, 2008), 127.

15 *Measuring Alpha in the Fund Management Industry: Do Female Managers Perform Better?* (2013 German Institute for Economic Research paper by Vassilis Babalos, Guglielmo Maria Caporale, and Nikolaos Philippas) concludes that male and female money managers have similar performance. *Women in Fund Management: A Road Map for Achieving Critical Mass—and Why It Matters* (The National Council for Research on Women, 2009) concludes: "In the largely homogenous, male-dominated world of investment management, men's tendency to assert dominance in aggressively risky decision-making is amplified and, in fact, helps explain the 'group think' or herd mentality noted by so many in the recent financial crisis." "Gender, Risk Tolerance, and False Consensus in Asset Allocation Recommendations" (2017 paper by Nicolas P.B. Bollen and Steven Posavac) found that while male students took more risk than their female peers, male and female wealth managers had similar risk preferences.

16 Sheelah Kolhatkar, "What If Women Ran Wall Street?," *New York*, March 21, 2010.

17 Enid Nemy and Catharine Rampell, "Muriel Siebert, a Determined Trailblazer for Women on Wall Street, Dies at 80," *New York Times*, August 26, 2013.

18 Myra MacPherson, *The Scarlet Sisters: Sex, Suffrage, and Scandal in the Gilded Age* (New York: Twelve, 2014), xxi.

19 Mary Gabriel, *Notorious Victoria: The Life of Victoria Woodhull, Uncensored* (Chapel Hill, NC: Algonquin Books, 1998), 39.

20 Grant Miller, *Women's Suffrage, Political Responsiveness, and Child Survival in American History, The Quarterly Journal of Economics* 123 no. 3 (August 1, 2008): 1287–1327.

21 Marcus Noland, Tyler Moran, and Barbara Kotschwar, "Is Gender Diversity Profitable? Evidence from a Global Survey," (Peterson Institute for International Economics Working Paper No. 16-3, February 2016).

22 Dividends comment from *The CS Gender 3000: Women in Senior Management* (Credit Suisse, September 2014), 20; bribery, corruption, and fraud from Linda-Eling Lee, Ric Marshall, Damion Rallis, and Matt Moscardi, *MSCI Women on Boards: Global Trends in Gender Diversity on Corporate Boards*, (MSCI, November 2015), 7.

23 Lyda Bigelow, Leif Lundmark, Judi McLean Parks, and Robert Wuebker, "Skirting the Issues: Experimental Evidence of Gender Bias in IPO Prospectus Evaluations," *Journal of Management* 40, no. 6 (September 2014): 1732–1759.

24 Lyda Bigelow, Leif Lundmark, Judi McLean Parks, and Robert Wuebker, "Skirting the Issues."

25 Alexandra Niessen-Ruenzi and Stefan Ruenzi, "Sex Matters: Gender and Prejudice in the Mutual Fund Industry" (paper, May 2013).

26 *Gender Diversity in Investment Management: New Research for Practitioners on How to Close the Gender Gap* (Charlottesville, VA: CFA Research Foundation, 2016).

27 Renée B. Adams, Brad M. Barber, and Terrance Odean, "Family, Values, and Women in Finance" (paper, September 2016).

Epilogue

1 Atul Gawande, *The Checklist Manifesto: How to Get Things Right* (New York: Metropolitan Books, 2010), 173.

2 Paul J. Zak, "Moral Markets," *Journal of Economic Behavior and Organization* (2011): 222.

3 Robert H. Frank, "The Status of Moral Emotions in Consequentialist Moral Reasoning," in *Moral Markets: The Critical Role of Values in the Economy*, ed. Paul J. Zak (Princeton: Princeton University Press, 2008), 46.

www.ingramcontent.com/pod-product-compliance
Ingram Content Group UK Ltd.
Pitfield, Milton Keynes, MK11 3LW, UK
UKHW042019190726
13854UKWH00005B/2372